Chinese Migrants Ageing in a Foreign Land

This book advances a new understanding of acculturation processes for older migrants, drawing on empirical data from migrants of Chinese heritage in Australia. It challenges the traditional models of acculturation, questions the conventional notion of integration, and analyses the fluid nature of cultural identities. Drawing on insights from environmental gerontology, intercultural communication and acculturation theories, it conceptualises ageing in a foreign land as a home-building process, highlighting the collective contributions of individual, community, social, cultural, technological and environmental factors to older migrants' well-being. A consideration of what it means to age "in place" for those whose home is not necessarily attached to one place and one culture, this volume will appeal to social scientists with interests in ageing, gerontology, migration and diaspora, as well as those working in the fields of aged care policy.

Shuang Liu is Associate Professor in the School of Communication and Arts at The University Queensland, Australia. She is the author of *Identity, Hybridity and Cultural Home: Chinese Migrants and Diaspora in Multicultural Societies* and the lead author of *Introducing Intercultural Communication: Global Cultures and Contexts*.

Chinese Migrants Ageing in a Foreign Land
Home Beyond Culture

Shuang Liu

LONDON AND NEW YORK

First published 2020
by Routledge
2 Park Square, Milton Park, Abingdon, Oxon OX14 4RN

and by Routledge
52 Vanderbilt Avenue, New York, NY 10017

Routledge is an imprint of the Taylor & Francis Group, an informa business

© 2020 Shuang Liu

The right of Shuang Liu to be identified as author of this work has been asserted by her in accordance with sections 77 and 78 of the Copyright, Designs and Patents Act 1988.

All rights reserved. No part of this book may be reprinted or reproduced or utilised in any form or by any electronic, mechanical, or other means, now known or hereafter invented, including photocopying and recording, or in any information storage or retrieval system, without permission in writing from the publishers.

Trademark notice: Product or corporate names may be trademarks or registered trademarks, and are used only for identification and explanation without intent to infringe.

British Library Cataloguing-in-Publication Data
A catalogue record for this book is available from the British Library

Library of Congress Cataloging-in-Publication Data
A catalog record has been requested for this book

ISBN: 978-0-367-21822-5 (hbk)
ISBN: 978-0-429-26632-4 (ebk)

Typeset in Times New Roman
by Apex CoVantage, LLC

Contents

List of figures	vi
Preface	vii

1	Ageing in a foreign land	1
2	Research context and methodology	19
3	Home as a place: physical insideness	37
4	Home as relationships: social and cultural insideness	55
5	Home as a transnational place: autobiographical insideness	73
6	Building a sense of home in a foreign land	92

Index	109

Figures

1.1 The Queenslander-style house is a classic piece of Australian architectural design, with its distinctive timber and corrugated iron appearance.   7

2.1 Chinatown Melbourne was established in the 1850s for Chinese gold seekers and has been an integral part of Melbourne.   22

2.2 Yum cha, involving Chinese tea and dim sum, is a popular Cantonese tradition for family and friends to gather together; the tradition is carried out worldwide where there are overseas Chinese communities.   25

3.1 Growing Asian vegetables in home gardens communicates a sense of home to older Chinese migrants in Australia.   41

3.2 Bus stations represent links between home and the outside world; the ability to get out and about by bus gives older Chinese migrants a feeling of being at home in Australia.   46

4.1 A certificate an older Chinese migrant made for her grandson to congratulate him on having mastered the skill of using chopsticks to eat meals, a Chinese tradition.   62

4.2 Chung Tian Temple, "Middle Heaven", in Brisbane is a place of worship for many Chinese migrants, particularly Buddhists.   66

5.1 Popular Chinese potato crackers, branded Shang Hao Jia, are sold in an Asian supermarket in Brisbane, Australia.   83

5.2 An older Chinese couple use an iPad and smartphones to keep connected with friends back in China.   86

6.1 Cathay Community Association, established in 1984, specialises in supporting older Asian migrants, mostly of Chinese heritage, to settle into a new life in Australia through regular respite social activities and home care services.   101

Preface

The impetus for writing this book emerged from my own experience as a Chinese migrant. Having lived in a foreign land for a significant part of my life, I have developed a profound interest in understanding how migrants develop a sense of home in a place where they may feel out of place due to cultural transition. When I first arrived in Brisbane for my job interview at The University of Queensland in 2000, I went to a coffee shop in the late afternoon before my interview. A young man at the counter greeted me with an enthusiastic, "G'day, how can I help you?" I asked for a coffee, to which he replied, "Sure, but what coffee?" I looked at the blackboard menu on the wall and was met with a dazzling list of coffee names that were all Greek to me. With something akin to performance anxiety, I quickly ordered, not entirely confident of what I was requesting. I ended up with a long black – double shots – which kept me awake till 2am the next morning. But I got the job!

Almost two decades have since passed, and I can now confidently order the right coffee in any café without having to look at a menu. Furthermore, I have learned to use Australian slang, formed a circle of Australian friends, equipped myself with knowledge about Australian culture, adopted an Australian lifestyle, and participated in events that are deemed Australian, such as watching the annual ANZAC Day parade. As a result, people around me often comment that I am an Australian. While I *am* an Australian citizen and I call Australia home, however, I do not *feel* Australian in the sense of the colour of my skin, the food I love, the values I treasure, the customs I observe, and many other things that have been transferred to me through my upbringing and my heritage culture. This incongruity has been the source of my questions and desire to learn more about the cultural experience of others similar to myself. How should people like me develop a sense of home in a foreign land, when home is not associated with one culture?

Over the past decade, I have conducted research on first and second generation Chinese migrants in Australia, as well as what is known as the "1.5"

viii *Preface*

generation – those people who migrated before they were 14 years of age. I have been drawn to gaining an understanding of how migrants define who they are as cultural beings, how they negotiate identities when discrepancies occur between their self-defined identity and identities ascribed to them by others, and how they develop a sense of belonging in the foreign land that they presently call home.

This book documents my more recent research, with a particular focus on older Chinese migrants. Most of them are at the age of 65 years or over, including both long-term Chinese migrants who have grown old in Australia, and those who moved to Australia at an older age. The participants I interviewed have various job backgrounds, ranging from businesspeople, chefs, shop-owners, doctors, homemakers, and teachers, to mention just a few. Through their stories and the photographs they shared with me, I have learned that, for older migrants, ageing in a foreign land is a complex acculturation journey that involves continuous integration with place and people in the context of change in personal, social, cultural, physical, and environmental circumstances. Even for those who made their migration journey at a young age and have grown old in Australia, the issue of identity and belonging remains. The older they grow, the more salient the question of cultural roots becomes. The Chinese saying goes, "Fallen leaves return to the roots". Because fallen leaves close to the roots of a tree will be absorbed by the soil and become part of the tree again, this saying is often used metaphorically to describe the nostalgic feeling and attachment to place of origin for those who live away from their homeland. For migrants, their heritage culture is always embedded in their lives, regardless of how long they have lived away from their homeland. The question of "culture" is not necessarily associated with one locality.

This book conceptualises ageing in a foreign land as a home-building process, drawing on theories of environmental gerontology, intercultural communication, and acculturation. It highlights the collective contributions of individual, community, social, cultural, technological and environmental factors to older migrants' well-being. Developing a sense of home in a foreign land is a core component of migrants' acculturation journey because cultural transition creates a feeling of being "out of place". Attachment to home is especially significant for older people due to their reduced levels of mobility and social engagement, the longer time they spend at home compared to younger people, and the importance of place in preserving a sense of independence in older age and well-being. Internationally, public health policies promote ageing in place, defined as older people living in their own homes and communities for as long as possible, instead of living in institutional care facilities, because of the associated benefits of being at one's own home. Some of these benefits include independence, familiarity

Preface ix

with the surrounding environment in the neighbourhood and community, and closer contact with family and friends. While we recognise that ageing in place is conducive to well-being and that a sense of home is especially important to older people, what we lack is scholarly discussions engaging with older migrants who are ageing outside their homeland.

This book advances new knowledge of the meaning of home through the eyes of Chinese migrants in Australia and delves into the fascinating processes through which they build a sense of home as they live and age in a foreign land. The fundamental question addressed is this: How do older Chinese migrants build a sense of home in a foreign land when home is not attached to one place, nor one culture? The concept of home is of special importance to older Chinese migrants because the Chinese culture has a long and strong tradition of family care. Many older Chinese migrants choose to live with their adult children and grandchildren under the same roof in Australia. Since younger Chinese generations tend to acculturate at a faster rate than older generations, an older Chinese migrant's home is, by extension, a cultural home. As such, home is a site where ethnic and mainstream cultures are traversed and where identity and a sense of belonging are negotiated. Moreover, this book challenges the traditional models of acculturation and questions the conventional notion that immigrant integration involves simultaneously maintaining heritage culture and participating in the national culture of the settlement country. The book argues that identity is a product of social construction; it is fluid, never fixed, and can be self-claimed as well as ascribed. Those who self-identify by a culture, be it ethnic or national, may not necessarily act in accordance with that culture, depending on the context. Furthermore, the novelty of this book lies in its interdisciplinary theoretical approach, which combines acculturation theories with environmental gerontology, whereby extending theories in both fields by using them to address problems beyond the confines of a single disciplinary area. In doing so, *Chinese Migrants Ageing in a Foreign Land: Home beyond culture* contributes to the broader debate on the dynamic relationships among place, people, and culture in the field of acculturation and gerontology.

In terms of practice, this book addresses an urgent problem that the world is facing globally, that is, enabling the increasingly diverse ageing population to age well. Although the empirical data and discussion of the findings here are based on older Chinese migrants in Australia, the implications drawn from the process-oriented and context-based research data apply to international contexts, including Asia, North America, and Europe. Added to the book's international appeal is the magnitude of the Chinese diaspora communities, which are the largest and most vibrant worldwide. This book offers new insights into when and how personal, community, social

x *Preface*

and cultural resources, physical facilities, and communication technologies can be best harnessed to help older people to age well in a foreign land. This knowledge can help to improve public policies in terms of informing community aged-care service providers in supplying effective and targeted support to suit the diverse cultural needs of older people. Therefore, when applied to policy and practice, these insights can improve the well-being of older Chinese migrants in particular, and that of the diverse ageing population in general.

I would like to thank all those who have helped me as I progressed through the journey of completing this book. A special note of thanks goes to the participants in my studies. They invited me into their world and shared their stories with me. These experiences have framed my outlook on the fascinating subject of building a home beyond culture. I thank the anonymous reviewers for their insightful comments on the book proposal and valuable suggestions for improvement. I am grateful to my colleagues and friends at The University of Queensland. In particular, I express my gratitude to: Emeritus Professor Cindy Gallois, for her encouragement during the early stages of the development of the book project, Emeritus Professor Graeme Turner, for his insightful suggestions on structuring the book; and Dr Siqin Wang, who assisted me in collecting data from participants and provided with me some photos to include in this book. I would like to thank the Faculty of Humanities and Social Sciences and the Institute for Advanced Studies in the Humanities at The University of Queensland for the fellowship between July and November of 2018, during which my book proposal was written.

My sincere appreciation goes to Mr Neil Jordan, the commissioning editor at Routledge. Without the encouragement, support and confidence he gave me, this book would not have come to fruition. Special thanks also go to the editorial assistant Ms Alice Salt, the production manager, and everyone from Routledge, Taylor & Francis Group, whose work has transformed the manuscript into its present form.

Finally, I am deeply indebted to my family for their support, love, and encouragement throughout the writing of this book.

1 Ageing in a foreign land

Introduction

The world is experiencing unprecedented growth in its ageing population, with the United Nations predicting the number of people aged 60 years or above to more than double from 2017 (962 million) to 2050 (2.1 billion), and then more than triple by 2100 (3.1 billion) (World Population, 2017). The UN report projects that by 2050 all regions of the world, except Africa, will have nearly a quarter of their population aged 60 and above. Further, the number of people from diverse cultural backgrounds aged 65 and over is increasing at a much faster speed than those of the same age range in the total population (World Migration Report, 2018). According to this report, older migrants aged 65 years and over account for 12% of migrants worldwide in 2017 compared to only 9% of people aged 65 years and over in the total population. Ageing well for older people of diverse backgrounds, therefore, will be the challenge facing researchers, practitioners, and policymakers in the years to come.

This chapter identifies various challenges facing older migrants who either made their migration journey at an older age or migrated at a relatively young age and grew old in the settlement country. Ageing in a foreign land creates a "double jeopardy" for older migrants as they deal with ageing as well as various challenges associated with cultural transition, such as loss of social networks and reduced level of independence due to language barriers (Neville, Wright-St Clair, Montayre, & Adams, 2018, p. 427). Ageing in a foreign land often creates a feeling of being "out of place". Rebuilding identity, attachment to place and a sense of belonging are core components of migrants' acculturation journey. This chapter conceptualises older migrants' acculturation as building a sense of "home" in the host country. A sense of home is especially important to older migrants because of both the longer time they spend at home compared to younger people and the key role of home in preserving independence in later life. As such, a feeling of

2 *Ageing in a foreign land*

being at home cultivates identity and a sense of belonging as older migrants age in a foreign land. Drawing on evidence from international research, this chapter highlights that, for migrants, home is not just a physical location and a set of relationships but, more importantly, it is a site where cultures are traversed, identities enacted, and belongings negotiated.

Challenges for older migrants

Internationally, government policies typically encourage older people to age in place, that is, to live and remain in their own home and community for as long as possible instead of living in a care facility (Frank, 2002). Research shows that ageing in place, compared to ageing within institutional care, is more conducive to older people's well-being because of associated benefits such as independence, familiarity with the neighbourhood and surrounding physical environment, closer contact with family, friends, and social networks, and the sense of comfort that comes from being in one's own home (Torres, 2013). However, with a significant proportion of the world's older population now being migrants, a sizable global population is, and will be, ageing outside their once familiar social, cultural, and physical environment. Besides those challenges routinely associated with ageing, doing so in a foreign land also brings with it social isolation (Lewicka, 2008), loneliness (Treas & Mazumdar, 2002), language barriers in the host country (Li, 2012), and low psychological well-being (Liu & Simpson Reeves, 2016). Despite the prevalence of these challenges, research on immigration to date has focused predominantly on younger generations, and older migrants have largely been ignored (Torres-Gil & Treas, 2008).

Broadly speaking, there are two categories of older migrants: those who migrated at a young age and grew old in their host country, and those who migrated at an older age for family reunification, usually to join their adult children who had settled down in the new host country before them. Older migrants who made the migration journey during their later years not only face the daunting challenge of leaving their familiar homeland and established social networks behind, but also have to tackle cross-cultural adjustment in a new country that is often different from their home country in culture, language, social systems, and lifestyles. Even those older migrants who moved to join their adult children often feel isolated from their younger family members because they cannot adjust to life in their new cultural environment as quickly as the younger people can. For those who migrated at a relatively young age, and thus grew old in a new country, things might not necessarily be easier. For example, in a number of studies involving older migrant groups who migrated at a young age and grew old in the United States, researchers found that older migrants from Korean, Chinese,

Ageing in a foreign land 3

Mexican, Russian, and Eastern European backgrounds are subject to higher health risks than non-migrants, often resulting from depressive symptoms (Chou, 2007). Clearly, older migrants experience unique stressors related to social isolation, loneliness, the loss of their social and cultural networks, language barriers, and intergenerational differences (Chow, 2004). Those stressors may not only hinder their capacity to age well in a foreign land, but also negatively impact their family and community. Resolution of this issue requires a rebuilding of identity, attachment to place, a sense of belonging, social networks, cultural connections, and intergenerational understanding.

The first key challenge older migrants face is building a sense of place. Research shows that many older migrants feel that they belong to neither their homeland, nor their settlement country (Meijering & Lager, 2014). Although this feeling of "being out of place" might be felt by migrants of all age groups, it tends to be stronger for older migrants because their social participation in both the old home culture and the new host culture is likely to decrease with ageing, and they become more dependent on others in their later years (Treas & Mazumdar, 2002). Attachment to place is important in fostering identity and belonging in older people's lives. A feeling of security and independence develops when an older person lives in a familiar neighbourhood, has the freedom to arrange his or her own furniture, and can choose to be surrounded by familiar memories (Dahlin-Ivanoff, Haak, Fänge, & Iwarsson, 2007). Moreover, place attachment extends to the neighbourhood and surrounding community (Wiles, Leibing, Guberman, Reeve, & Allen, 2012). For example, public spaces such as footpaths or parks may have emotional or social meanings for older people. A study by Ottoni and colleagues (2016) found that park benches and outdoor seating areas in public places are important to the health and well-being of older people in terms of reducing social isolation because they provide areas for them to relax and connect with others. Although Ottoni and colleagues's (2016) research did not specifically focus on migrants, their research findings shed light on the importance of place attachment for older migrants' well-being.

The second key challenge older migrants face is rebuilding cultural identity and a sense of belonging in their host country. When cultural transition occurs, a migrant's sense of belonging usually needs to be reconstructed for their new cultural context. Cultural identity is one's essential experience of self, and it encompasses the worldview, values, history, and beliefs an individual shares with his or her cultural group. A strong cultural identity imparts to an individual a sense of belonging to a stable and identifiable cultural group, and provides a frame of reference for thinking, doing, and being (Butler-Sweet, 2011). In its most manifest form, cultural identity both locates a person within a cultural group and differentiates the person from

4   Ageing in a foreign land

other cultural groups. The categories people use to define themselves culturally, for example, Chinese or Australian, symbolically mark the boundaries between the self and the other. Indeed, the attachment and pride of belonging to a cultural group is essential in forming a solid foundation for psychological well-being (Berry, 1997). On the other hand, lacking a sense of belonging has been found to lead to a feeling of cultural homelessness among migrants (Walters & Auton-Cuff, 2009), as well as a perception of reduced control over one's life (Zhan, Wang, Fawcett, Li, & Fan, 2017). While migrants derive a sense of belonging from identifying with their original culture, they are also fully aware that this very identification with "where you're from" is also an indication of being an outsider in the place of "where you're at" (Ang, 2001, p. 34). Hence, reconstructing cultural identity and belonging is an ongoing process migrants undergo as they live in the host country.

The third key challenge that older migrants face is the language barriers that prevent them from connecting with the larger society and make their cross-cultural adjustment more difficult. For example, Park and Kim's (2013) study on elderly Korean people in New Zealand illustrates that a lack of understanding of the English language and of New Zealand culture significantly contributed to participants feeling disconnected from the community, which led to their reduced participation in the available social activities. A participant who could not speak English well expressed, "I felt becoming deaf, blind and mute after immigration, and living in an inconvenient paradise" (Park & Kim, 2013, p. 159). Similarly, Li's 2012 study on older Chinese migrants in New Zealand found that perceived language and cultural barriers limited migrants' ability to participate in social activities and contributed to them feeling out of place, lonely, and confined to their homes. Learning the language of their host country can be a daunting challenge for those who migrated at an older age. Even those who have lived in the host country for decades may still have difficulties in using the national language of the host country. Longer duration of residence does not always translate into a higher level of national language proficiency, although it may facilitate learning the national language of the host country.

The fourth key challenge older migrants face is negotiating cultural differences in intergenerational relationships. Due to their primary socialisation occurring in their home country, first generation migrants often arrive in the host country with an established set of ideas regarding family relations, cultural beliefs, and adherence to customs and traditions. Those culturally informed ideas often result in culture-specific assumptions about aged care, particularly the role that the younger generations are expected to play in that care. Cultural isolation and linguistic difficulties increase older migrants' dependence on their children and diminish the probability

Ageing in a foreign land   5

of older migrants seeking assistance from formal care providers in their host country. Moreover, many older migrants from Asian backgrounds are economically dependent on their children to some extent, and are reluctant to access formal care for fear it could be viewed as familial rejection (Chow, 2004). However, generational differences in the adherence or otherwise to traditional cultural values and practices can lead to problems in intergenerational relationships. For example, research on Asian migrants in Western countries shows significant departures from the Confucian tradition of filial piety (the virtue of respect for one's elders and caring for one's elderly parents). While the older generation expects to be cared for by the younger generation, their adult children tend to see filial piety more in terms of provision of financial support to their elderly parents than in being a personal carer (Gui & Koropeckyj-Cox, 2016). As a result, discrepancies in views of family care held by the older and the younger generations can create barriers in intergenerational relationships.

Acculturation as a home-building process

The identified challenges that older migrants face are an integral part of their acculturation journey in the host country. Acculturation refers to a process of change arising from sustained contact between cultures (Redfield, Linton, & Herskovits, 1936). Much of the acculturation theorising relies on Berry's (1997) fourfold model that defines acculturation as the process by which change occurs in migrants because of contact with their host culture and participation in their host society; such change could be reflected in their orientation to both the old culture and the new culture. Although acculturation occurs in both migrants and host nationals due to contact between cultures, this book focuses on migrants' acculturation. According to Berry's (1997) model of acculturation, migrants are confronted with two basic questions which centre on the maintenance of their original ethnic culture, and their connections with the host society. Mapping answers to these two questions generates four different acculturation strategies: integration, assimilation, separation, and marginalisation. Migrants who favour ethnic cultural maintenance and at the same time express interest in becoming an integral part of their host society are called integrationists. Those who attach low significance to maintaining ethnic culture and only view themselves as members of the host society adopt the assimilation strategy. Migrants who desire ethnic cultural maintenance but do not wish to establish contact with their host culture are called separationists. Those who desire neither ethnic cultural maintenance nor contact with their host culture adopt the marginalisation strategy. Previous studies have found integration to be the most common acculturation strategy among migrants, followed by assimilation

6 Ageing in a foreign land

and separation. Marginalisation is usually shown to be the least preferred (Ward & Geeraert, 2016). In many contexts and places, integration has been found to be related to positive acculturation outcomes. This is defined as a combination of psychological well-being (e.g., life satisfaction) and sociocultural adjustment (e.g., making new friends). Intercultural scholars argue that adoption of the integration strategy allows immigrants to develop material and emotional connections to their new culture, while still maintaining ties to their original ethnic culture (Berry, Phinney, Sam, & Vedder, 2006). Many acculturation researchers recognise integration as beneficial because integrating two cultures within oneself allows movement between cultures without feeling disoriented (LaFromboise, Coleman, & Gerton, 1993). However, there have also been studies showing that simply identifying with both old and new cultures does not always lead to successful integration and can even result in identity conflict (Berry & Sabatier, 2011). The reason is that the process of dealing with more than one culture and acquiring more than one behavioural repertoire can cause stress, isolation, and identity confusion (Benet-Martínez, 2012). An international meta-analysis based on 83 studies and over 23,000 participants indicates that findings are inconsistent with regard to the direction and magnitude of the association between biculturalism and cross-cultural adjustment (Nguyen & Benet-Martinez, 2013). These mixed findings highlight the complexity of the acculturation process, particularly given that a migrants' choice of acculturation strategy can change across time and context. Therefore, to elucidate the mixed findings in the literature, we need more research on how integration is understood and experienced from migrants' perspectives, as well as how "it unfolds over time and what are the underlying dynamics of integration" (Ward, 2013, p. 394).

At the fundamental level, integration is about identity and belonging: who we are culturally, and how we relate to people in our own cultural group and those in other cultural groups (Berry et al., 2006). Culture provides a frame of reference for both self-concept and social relationships (Berry, 1997). As members of a cultural group interact with each other to establish consensual meanings of their shared experiences, they come to agree on what is important to their culture. Over time, such collective agreements become shared knowledge, which forms the common ground that members of the same cultural group use as the basis for self-identification and as a guide for social behaviours. This common ground also informs the evaluation of the appropriateness of the words and actions of their own group members and others who are not members of their cultural group. Therefore, culture marks group boundaries and cultural differences separate people from people. The question of difference is emotive: friend versus foe, belonging versus not belonging, and us versus them. Decisions relating to all of those aspects have an emotional component (Clarke, 2008). The question of how migrants develop a sense of cultural identity and belonging has been central to over five decades of acculturation research (Ward & Geeraert, 2016). As cultural transition for migrants often creates a feeling of being out of place due to loss of connections with place and people in the once familiar home cultural context, we conceptualise acculturation as a process of building a sense of home in their host country. The concept of home in a foreign land captures multiple meanings embedded in place, objects, and people. The development of a sense of home in the place where people reside is a prerequisite to a sense of identity and belonging (Lewicka, 2008).

Photo 1.1 The Queenslander-style house is a classic piece of Australian architectural design, with its distinctive timber and corrugated iron appearance.

Source: Shuang Liu. Used with permission.

8 *Ageing in a foreign land*

As a physical place, home is "a defined space for its residents providing shelter and protection for domestic activities and concealment, and an entity separating private from public domains" (Oswald & Wahl, 2005, p. 21). "Home" entails physical amenities, functionality such as furniture arrangement, and the ways in which family members engage with those functionalities within the home. However, studies on older people have consistently shown that home is much more than its physical location or functionality; home evokes strong social and personal meaning, which can positively influence the well-being of older people (Sixsmith, 1986). As such, an increasing number of researchers have looked also at the emotional and cultural significance of place, and its effect on identity and well-being (Lewin, 2001). For example, a study in the Netherlands found that older people place great value on the intangible aspects of place, including their lived experiences, cultural traditions, memories, and life stories, when developing a feeling of belonging in their host country (van Hees, Horstman, Jansen, & Ruwaard, 2017). In this sense, home is not simply a location, but a "warehouse of memories" connecting their old life in their homeland with new life in the host country (Stones & Gullifer, 2016, p. 458). This study further shows that familiarity with the neighbourhood and freedom to travel to nearby facilities by public transport can give older people a sense of independence and control over their lives. Hence, home extends beyond the house to the surrounding communities (Wiles et al., 2012).

As a social place, home entails a set of relationships within a shared space, such as relationships with family and friends. Family relations and intergenerational relationships play a pivotal role in making people feel at home. Research shows that older migrants contribute to family by enhancing intergenerational relationships and maintaining or promoting the culture of their homeland. For example, older Chinese migrants in the US undertake childcare and household responsibilities because they believe that this tradition develops bonds between generations in the family (Zhang & Zhan, 2009). It is emotionally comforting for older migrants to be with family members who share their cultural heritage, speak their ethnic language, observe their traditional practices, such as celebrating festivals and eating traditional foods, and pass those practices on from generation to generation (Hoersting & Jenkins, 2011). This argument is supported by a qualitative study exploring how older Chinese migrants conceptualise the notion of home. In that study, Liangni Liu (2014) found that participants experience emotional comfort when they are with family members who share a cultural heritage. Conversely, other researchers have found that older Chinese are more likely to experience intergenerational cultural differences because it is common practice for older Chinese to live with their adult children and grandchildren in their host country (Zhang & Zhan, 2009). Many older

Chinese people hold a strong view on the traditional family-care practice in Chinese culture whereby it is the duty of younger generations to act as personal carers for elderly members of the family when needed. Elderly family members living in a nursing home would indicate a lack of filial piety on the part of their adult children (Gui & Koropeckyj-Cox, 2016). The Chinese saying, "Raise children for the purpose of being looked after in old age" (*yang er fang lao*), reflects these cultural expectations. On the other hand, younger generations may not accept these expectations, and may see their filial piety more in terms of financial support than hands-on care (Mui & Kang, 2006). Therefore, home for older migrants is a social space where cultural identity and belonging are negotiated through intergenerational relationships and intergenerational understanding.

Home for older migrants can be a transnational space because often their home is a combination of their old home in their homeland and their new home in their settlement country. Baffoe (2009) found that African migrants living in Montreal, Toronto, and Winnipeg maintained emotional and cultural connections to their homeland by recreating aspects of their home culture. They did this by displaying cultural artefacts, eating cultural foods, and joining cultural groups in their community. Similarly, a study by Liu (2015) on first and second generation Chinese migrants in Australia reinforced the importance of traditional food and cultural artefacts in maintaining cultural continuity. Blunt and Dowling (2006, p. 199) described this process of cultural continuity in the host country as "home-making practice", which assists migrants to engage in the dynamic interactions between their homeland and the foreign land. Such cultural connections can be made across geographic borders thanks to communication technologies. Through internet-enabled devices such as computers, tablets, and mobile phones, and through social media, many older migrants keep in contact with their old social circles, access news in their ethnic language via satellite television programs from their home country, ethnic newspapers, and social media platforms. Regardless of where they have migrated to and how long they have resided in their host country, migrants' homes in their host countries are always imbued with their home culture.

The person-environment model

The importance of home to older people has been studied in various disciplinary areas. Despite the disciplinary variations, one consensus among scholars is that ageing occurs in context. Context can cover physical, social, cultural, and personal domains as well as a myriad of others. Researchers from different areas concentrate on the impact of specific domains on older people as they undergo ageing processes. Social and behavioural sciences

10 *Ageing in a foreign land*

in particular have emphasised the roles of historical, cultural, and social contexts in shaping ageing processes(Wahl & Oswald, 2010). A number of social gerontology studies have placed emphasis on the crucial influence of physical surroundings on older people. Consequently, environmental gerontology has emerged as a sub-discipline of the developing area of social gerontology (Wahl & Oswald, 2010). Theorising in environmental gerontology starts with the fundamental idea that development over a person's life span, including old age, is driven by an ongoing interchange between that person and his or her social and physical environments (Oswald & Wahl, 2005). Environmental gerontology, therefore, aims to describe, explain, and modify or optimise the relationship between an ageing person and his or her physical-social environment. Such research advances an in-depth understanding of the relationships between ageing persons and their physical-social environments, as well as how those relationships influence a variety of outcomes for older people, such as identity, autonomy, and well-being (Wahl & Gitlin, 2007). Although this research tradition was significantly expanded between the 1960s and 1980s, it rarely engaged with older migrants.

Viewed through the lens of environmental gerontology, home is "physically, psychologically, and socially constructed" (Sommerville, 1997, p. 226). From the moment of birth and throughout their lifespan, people interact with surrounding environment, be it physical, social, or cultural. As people grow older, their home environment becomes more important because of the significant amount of time older people spend at home and in its immediate surroundings as their social participation decreases (Oswald & Wahl, 2005). Environmental gerontology argues that attachment to home and place is especially significant for older people's well-being because of not only the longer time spent there, but also the significance of place in preserving a sense of identity, belonging, and independence in old age (Oswald & Wahl, 2005). Consequently, we see research examining both the objective and subjective processes of older people interacting with their environments. Research on the objective dimensions of their environment has primarily focused on the control older people have over design characteristics of their houses and on the demands of physical environments (Steinfeld & Danford, 1999). Other studies have explored the relationship between attachment to place and a sense of belonging, identity, and quality of life (Sixsmith, 1986). It needs to be noted that environmental gerontology recognises the necessity of an interdisciplinary understanding of person-environment interchange processes because there is no objective environment that is not subject to social and cultural interpretation (Wahl & Oswald, 2010).

Using a social-geographical approach, Graham Rowles (1983) conceptualises the person-environment relationship in terms of three dimensions

Ageing in a foreign land 11

of insideness: physical insideness, social insideness, and autobiographical insideness. Physical insideness refers to an older person's familiarity with physical facilities and services in the neighbourhood. This comes from routines within that environment such as walking to local shops, visiting the doctor, resting in the local park, accessing public transport, and visiting friends. Social insidedness focuses on an older person's integration into the community, social networks, and culture. This involves everyday contact with people in social networks, including communication in person or through the internet. Such contact leads to connectedness with the community and culture, a sense of belonging, and an identification with place (Buffel, 2017). Moreover, strong ties to neighbours and friends can facilitate an older person's access to informal support and attenuate possible negative impacts of social isolation on health. Autobiographical insidedness is derived from a sense of identity that an older person has developed over time through the cumulative experiences of living in a place, leading to an emotional bond with the place. The creation of identity through autobiographical insideness provides a continuity between the past and the present (Wahl & Oswald, 2010).

This "three insideness framework" was based on Rowles' three years of participant observation research with elderly residents in Colton, a declining Appalachian community. The aim of his research was to understand the interchange of person-environment for older people and how such interrelations influence their ageing experiences. Commencing in 1978, the study involved observation of a panel of 15 elderly Colton residents, aged 62–91, and interviews with 32 elderly persons. The findings show that a feeling of social insideness, arising from the participants' integration with the social fabric of the community, complements their familiarity with the physical environment. For example, those participants who belonged to a social group called *The Society of the Old* derived both social support and a sense of belonging from integration with this social network. Social insideness, in turn, translates into attachment to physical place (Rowles, 1983). As autobiographic insideness embraces not only the present place but also remembered places linking the past with the present, it can serve as an extension of the old self to the new environment.

The three dimensions of insideness are not mutually exclusive, as Rowles (1983) suggests. Rather, they represent complementary aspects of a central rubric governing older people's person-environment interchange processes. Moreover, the three insideness dimensions may not develop at the same speed. An older person may be able to establish physical insideness with a new environment after living there for a period of time, then subsequently develop social insideness as new social networks develop. However, autobiographical insideness within their new physical and social environment

12 *Ageing in a foreign land*

may take longer to develop "due to the need to accumulate a reservoir of memorable incidents within the new environment" (Rowles, 1983, p. 310). Another interesting observation made by Rowles' study is that autobiographical insideness may be transferred through artefacts or objects (e.g., old furniture from home country being shipped to the new home in the host country) as a means of extending the old self into the new environment, whereby preserving identity continuity. The processes through which the three dimensions of insideness develop and interact with one another shed light on our understanding of the meaning of home to older people, particularly those who undergo relocation from a familiar environment to an unfamiliar one, as well as their coping strategies in the context of change in the environment.

Despite its relevance to understanding older migrants' ageing experiences, research from environmental gerontology engaging with migrants who move across cultures is very limited. Hence, the two strands of literature, acculturation and environmental gerontology, have often been kept separate in research on ageing people (Buffel, 2017). Nevertheless, we have seen some more recent attempts that apply environmental gerontology theorising to understand the acculturation processes through which older migrants re-establish insideness in their new cultural context. For example, Buffel (2017) combined environmental gerontology with works in transnational migration in order to identify the ways in which ageing migrants experience and create the notion of home, both as a location and a set of relationships. Drawing on data from 34 interviews with first generation Turkish migrants living in inner-city districts of Brussels, the study explores various ways in which older Turkish labour migrants build a sense of home that fosters feelings of identity and belonging. The findings show that the older Turkish migrants experience and create home as a site of connection within and across communities, reflecting a feeling of transnational belonging. By engaging in everyday social interactions with people in the community, establishing and using ethnic amenities such as mosques, and maintaining networks within their neighbourhood and families, the Turkish older participants in the study transformed their neighbourhood into a transnational social space, which connected their home country with their host country. Such practices enabled those older Turkish migrants to create a sense of home, identity, and belonging in their new cultural context.

Of the three dimensions of insideness, social insideness seems to have attracted more attention from scholars than physical or autobiographical insideness, as documented in the literature. In the case of migrants, the concept of social insideness needs to incorporate cultural connectedness as well. Loss of social and cultural connections is a key challenge experienced by older migrants including those who moved to their host country to

Ageing in a foreign land 13

join their family because migration means that they have left their familiar social networks and culture behind. Rebuilding old social networks in a new country is often more difficult for older migrants than younger ones, due to their reduced level of physical mobility. This puts older migrants at elevated risk for social isolation (Treas & Mazumdar, 2002). One reason may be that many older people aged 65 years or above are no longer in the workforce, which is a common place for developing social networks. Active social participation is a means to enhance social connectedness and reduce social isolation, as well as receiving social support. An illustration of the importance of social connectedness to well-being comes from a study on older Chinese migrants in Canada (Martin-Matthews, Tong, Rosenthal, & McDonald, 2013). The participants found community support for their cultural adjustment in Chinese religious communities and Tai-Chi groups. The study argues that accessing social groups involving members and activities from older Chinese migrants' heritage culture facilitates integration, whereby a sense of home is developed in a foreign land.

To promote social participation, the World Health Organisation (WHO) launched *Global Age-Friendly Cities: A guide* (2007): a report that emphasises the importance of age-friendly communities in enabling social participation and active ageing. This report was the result of inviting older people from 33 cities worldwide to determine the importance of aspects of an age-friendly city. Taking the initiative further, Wiles and colleagues (2012) conducted focus groups and interviews with 121 participants, aged from 56 to 92 years to learn about what ageing in place means from the perspectives of immigrants themselves. Unlike the WHO project which presented eight topics (ranging from housing and transportation to respect and social inclusion), Wiles and colleagues' (2012) study adopted a more participatory approach, by asking open questions to let the older people define the meaning of "ageing in place" in their own words (Wiles et al., 2012, p. 359). The findings elucidated the pragmatic nature of place attachment, which participants described experiencing simply by being greeted as they walked down the street and by knowing where the local supermarket is. Such everyday routines provide older people with evidence of belonging to the community and familiarity with the place and people. Neville and colleagues (2018) reviewed studies on inclusive communities for older migrants by analysing ten peer-reviewed journal articles published in English after 2007, the year the WHO report was published. The findings indicate that limited host language ability is a significant barrier to building social insideness. Despite these recent attempts to research older migrants, there is still relatively limited applications of the person-environment model in environmental gerontology theorising to address social participation of older migrants (Torres, 2013).

14   *Ageing in a foreign land*

Nevertheless, previous research on immigration consistently shows that home is a constant process involving ongoing negotiations of meaning, old and new cultures, identity, and belonging. The physical, social, and psychological aspects of the home operate in interconnected ways. Although most discussions on ageing in place focus on home as a physical space, there is a growing recognition in environmental gerontology that the concept of home extends into the surrounding neighbourhood and community, which are crucial in older people's ability to age well. Oftentimes, it is the subjective feeling of a neighbourhood or the immediate social and cultural environment that provides a person with a significant source of satisfaction with life, regardless of objective measures of the functionality of a place. Therefore, ageing well in place is not just about attachment to a particular place; more importantly, it involves an older person's capacity to continually integrate with place and people in the context of change in their personal, social, cultural, and physical environments (Wiles et al., 2012). To understand the dynamics of ageing experiences, we need to explore what ageing in place means to older people in their own words and in context. Such an approach is in line with environmental gerontologists' call for more participatory research *with* older people rather than *on* them (Scheidt & Windley, 2006).

Conclusion

This chapter has identified key challenges older migrants face in relation to rebuilding social networks, a sense of place, familiarity with their new cultural environment, and the negotiation of identities within themselves and with younger generations in their families. Drawing on evidence from international research, this chapter has illustrated that home for older migrants is a multifaceted concept, which is evolving through interactions among physical place, objects, intergenerational relationships, and social connections including transnational networks. Since culture for migrants is not associated with one place, migrants continuously negotiate their sense of home between their old and new worlds and thus forge novel configurations of identification with home in both places as they become more familiar with the once unfamiliar host country. It is, therefore, imperative for acculturation researchers to delve into the nuanced ways in which migrants continue to build a sense of home as their life straddles their old country and the new host country.

As the concept of home is multi-layered, ranging from psychological to physical to social domains, diverse perspectives on home-building in a foreign land are especially needed to understand how connections with multiple places are integrated in the ageing experiences of older migrants. Many variables including age, gender, living arrangement, length of residence in

Ageing in a foreign land 15

their host country, health, social roles, education, income, and social support contribute to the ageing experiences of older migrants. Furthermore, as ageing in place is a complex process, we need more studies using integrated theoretical approaches to drill down into the process of building a sense of home and to understand how such processes influence migrants' ability to age well in a foreign land. Although acculturation theorising and environmental gerontology both interrogate the concept of home for older migrants, they have been kept separate in studies of ageing experiences. This chapter has demonstrated the applicability of an integrated theoretical approach to understanding ageing in a foreign land.

Attachment to the place where older people live is particularly significant for them due to the amount of time they spend in their own homes. In this context, home plays an important role in creating a sense of belonging, as well as preserving a sense of identity and independence in later life (Buffel, 2017). For older migrants, home has physical as well as social and cultural components, such as upholding traditional values and beliefs, eating traditional food, speaking their ethnic language, passing on their old culture to younger generations, maintaining intergenerational relationships, and negotiating intergenerational understanding. When place is explored as more than a geographical location, the research promotes a deeper understanding of ageing in place. As Wiles and colleagues (2012, p. 358) state, building a sense of place is "not merely about attachment to a particular home but where the older person is continually reintegrating with places and renegotiating meanings and identity in the face of dynamic landscapes of social, political, cultural, and personal change".

Population aging is a worldwide phenomenon, and the ageing population will continue to increase in the years to come. Global trends of international migration have resulted in a sizable population aging outside of their place of origin. This demographic shift has created challenges for individuals, communities, families, community aged care service providers, and policy makers to understand and support older people to age well. Despite a plethora of literature that exists within the acculturation scholarship highlighting the importance of building a sense of home to migrants' well-being, very few studies have advanced our understanding of the meaning of home for older migrants themselves and what they do to build a sense of home in a foreign land (Zhan et al., 2017). Currently, there is a very limited amount of research that explores the lived experiences of older migrants, and how they build a sense of home. Much of previous research theorises the home-building process for older people within one cultural context, with very limited research focusing on the home-building process from the perspectives of older migrants. This book generates insight into this under-researched area by exploring the home-building process for older Chinese migrants

16   *Ageing in a foreign land*

in Australia. Such research will enrich our understanding of how home is experienced both as a location and as a set of relationships among older migrants ageing in a foreign land. The next chapter details the research context and methodology.

References

Ang, I. (2001). *On not speaking Chinese: Living between Asia and the West*. London: Routledge.

Baffoe, M. (2009). The social reconstruction of "home" among African immigrants in Canada. *Canadian Ethnic Studies, 41–42*(3–1), 157–173.

Benet-Martínez, V. (2012). Multiculturalism: Cultural, social, and personality processes. In K. Deaux & M. Snyder (Eds.), *Oxford handbook of personality and social psychology* (pp. 623–648). Oxford: Oxford University Press.

Berry, J. W. (1997). Immigration, acculturation, and adaptation. *Applied Psychology, 46*, 5–34.

Berry, J. W., Phinney, J. S., Sam, D. L., & Vedder, P. (2006). Immigrant youth: Acculturation, identity, and adaptation. *Applied Psychology, 55*(3), 303–332.

Berry, J. W., & Sabatier, C. (2011). Variations in the assessment of acculturation attitudes: Their relationships with psychological wellbeing. *International Journal of Intercultural Relations, 35*, 658–699.

Blunt, A., & Dowling, R. (2006). *Home*. Abingdon: Routledge.

Buffel, T. (2017). Ageing migrants and the creation of home: Mobility and the maintenance of transnational ties. *Population, Space and Place, 23*(5), doi:10.1002/psp.1994

Butler-Sweet, C. (2011). Race isn't what defines me: Exploring identity choices in transracial, biracial, and monoracial families. *Social Identities, 17*, 747–769.

Chou, K. L. (2007). Psychological distress in migrants in Australia over 50 years old: A longitudinal investigation. *Journal of Affective Disorders, 98*(1–2), 99–108.

Chow, N. (2004). Asian value and aged care. *Geriatrics and Gerontology International, 4*(1), 21–25.

Clarke, S. (2008). Culture and identity. In T. Bennettt & J. Frow (Eds.), *The Sage handbook of cultural analysis* (pp. 510–529). London: Sage.

Dahlin-Ivanoff, S., Haak, M., Fänge, A., & Iwarsson, S. (2007). The multiple meaning of home as experienced by very old Swedish people. *Scandinavian Journal of Occupational Therapy, 14*(1), 25–32.

Frank, J. B. (2002). *The paradox of aging in place in assisted living*. London: Bergin & Garvey.

Gui, T., & Koropeckyj-Cox, T. (2016). "I am the only child of my parents": Perspectives on future elder care for parents among Chinese only-children living overseas. *Journal of Cross-Cultural Gerontology, 31*, 255–275.

Hoersting, R. C., & Jenkins, S. R. (2011). No place to call home: Cultural homelessness, self-esteem and cross-cultural identities. *International Journal of Intercultural Relations, 35*, 17–30.

LaFromboise, T., Coleman, H. L., & Gerton, J. (1993). Psychological impact of biculturalism: Evidence and theory. *Psychological Bulletin, 114*(3), 395–412.

Ageing in a foreign land 17

Lewicka, M. (2008). Place attachment, place identity, and place memory: Restoring the forgotten city past. *Journal of Environmental Psychology, 28*, 209–231.

Lewin, F. A. (2001). The meaning of home among elderly immigrants: Directions for future research and theoretical development. *Housing Studies, 16*(3), 353–370.

Li, W. (2012). Art in health and identity: Visual narratives of older Chinese immigrants to New Zealand. *Arts & Health, 4*(2), 109–123.

Liu, L. S. (2014). A search for a place to call home: Negotiations of home, identity and sense of belonging among new migrants from the People's Republic of China (PRC) to New Zealand. *Emotions, Space and Society, 10*, 18–26.

Liu, S. (2015). In search for a sense of place: Identity negotiation of Chinese immigrants. *International Journal of Intercultural Relations, 46*, 26–35.

Liu, S., & Simpson Reeves, L. (2016). Migration and aging. In N. Pachana (Ed.), *Encyclopedia of geropsychology*. Singapore: Springer. doi:10.1007/978-981-287-080-3_292–1

Martin-Matthews, A., Tong, C., Rosenthal, J., & McDonald, L. (2013). Ethnic cultural diversity in the experience of widowhood in later life: Chinese widows in Canada. *Journal of Ageing Studies, 27*(4), 507–518.

Meijering, L., & Lager, D. (2014). Home-making of older Antillean migrants in the Netherlands. *Ageing & Society, 34*, 859–875.

Mui, A. C., & Kang, S-Y. (2006). Acculturation stress and depression among Asian immigrant elders. *Social Work, 51*(3), 243–255.

Neville, S., Wright-St Clair, V., Montayre, J., Adams, J., & Larmer, P. (2018). Promoting age-friendly communities: An integrative review of inclusion for older immigrants. *Journal of Cross-Cultural Gerontology, 33*, 427–440.

Nguyen, A., & Benet-Martinez, V. (2013). Biculturalism and adjustment: A meta-analysis. *Journal of Cross-Cultural Psychology, 44*(1), 122–159.

Oswald, F., & Wahl, H. W. (2005). Dimensions of the meaning of home in later life. In G. D. Rowles & H. Chaudhury (Eds.), *Home and identity in late life: International perspectives* (pp. 21–45). New York, NY: Springer.

Ottoni, C., Sims-Gould, J., Winters, M., Heijnen, M., & McKay, H. (2016). "Benches become like porches": Built and social environment influences on older adults' experiences of mobility and well-being. *Social Sciences and Medicine, 169*, 33–41.

Park, H-J., & Kim, C. (2013). Ageing in an inconvenient paradise: The immigrant experiences of older Korean people in New Zealand. *Australasian Journal of Ageing, 32*, 168–162.

Redfield, R., Linton, R., & Herskovits, M. (1936). Memorandum for the study of acculturation. *American Anthropologist, 38*, 149–152.

Rowles, G. D. (1983). Place and personal identity in old age: Observations from Appalachia. *Journal of Environmental Psychology, 3*, 299–313.

Scheidt, R. J., & Windley, P. G. (2006). Environmental gerontology: Progress in post-Lawton era. In J. E. Birren & K. W. Schaie (Eds.), *Handbook of the psychology of aging* (6th ed., pp. 105–125). Burlington, MA: Elsevier.

Sixsmith, J. A. (1986). The meaning of home: An exploratory study in environmental experience. *Journal of Environmental Psychology, 6*, 281–298.

18 Ageing in a foreign land

Sommerville, P. (1997). The social construction of home. *Journal of Architectural and Planning Research, 14*, 227–245.

Steinfeld, E., & Danford, G. S. (Eds.). (1999). *Enabling environments: Measuring the impact of environment on disability and rehabilitation.* New York, NY: Plenum.

Stones, D., & Gullifer, J. (2016). "At home it's just so much easier to be yourself": Older adults' perceptions of ageing in place. *Ageing & Society, 36*, 449–481.

Torres, S. (2013). Transnationalism and the study of aging and old age. In C. Phellas (Ed.), *Aging in European societies* (pp. 267–281). New York, NY: Springer.

Torres-Gil, F., & Treas, J. (2008). Immigration and aging: The nexus of complexity and promise. *Generation, 32*(4), 6–10.

Treas, J., & Mazumdar, S. (2002). Older people in America's immigrant families: Dilemmas of dependence, integration, and isolation. *Journal of Aging Studies, 16*, 243–258.

van Hees, S., Horstman, K., Jansen, M., & Ruwaard, D. (2017). Photovoicing the neighbourhood: Understanding the situated meaning of intangible places for ageing-in-place. *Health & Place, 48*, 11–19.

Wahl, H-W., & Gitlin, L. N. (2007). Environmental gerontology. In J. E. Birren (Ed.), *Encyclopedia of gerontology: Age, ageing and the aged* (2nd ed., pp. 494–501). Oxford: Elsevier.

Wahl, N-W., & Oswald, F. (2010). Environmental perspectives on ageing. In D. Dannefer & C. Phillipson (Eds.), *The Sage handbook of social gerontology* (pp. 111–124). London: Sage.

Walters, K. A., & Auton-Cuff, F. P. (2009). A story to tell: The identity development of women growing up as third culture kids. *Mental Health, Religion & Culture, 12*(7), 755–772.

Ward, C. (2013). Probing identity, integration and adaptation. *International Journal of Intercultural Relations, 37*, 391–401.

Ward, C., & Geeraert, N. (2016). Advancing acculturation theory and research: The acculturation process in its ecological context. *Current Opinion in Psychology, 8*, 98–104.

Wiles, J. L., Leibing, A., Guberman, N., Reeve, J., & Allen, R. E. S. (2012). The meaning of "ageing in place" to older people. *The Gerontologist, 52*(3), 357–366.

World Migration Report. (2018). The UN migration agency. Retrieved from http://publications.iom.int/system/files/pdf/wmr_2018_en.pdf.

World Population. (2017). World population projected to reach 9.8 billion in 2050, and 11.2 billion in 2100. Retrieved from www.un.org/development/desa/en/key-issues/population.html.

Zhan, H., Wang, Q., Fawcett, Z., Li, X., & Fan, X. (2017). Finding a sense of home across the Pacific in old age: Chinese American senior's report of life satisfaction in a foreign land. *Journal of Cross Cultural Gerontology, 32*, 31–55.

Zhang, G., & Zhan, H. J. (2009). Beyond the bible and the cross: A social and cultural analysis of Chinese elders' participation in Christian congregation in the United States. *Sociological Spectrum, 29*(2), 295–317.

2 Research context and methodology

Introduction

Significant flows of migrants have made the Australia of today one of the most culturally diverse countries in the world. Since 1945, when the country's immigration department was established, it has become the home to more than seven million migrants (Parliament of Australia, 2010). Today, over 200 different languages are spoken in Australia, and more than one in five of the Australian population speak a language other than English at home (Australian Bureau of Statistics [ABS], 2016). As Castles (1992, p. 549) points out, nowhere is this more apparent than in a country like Australia, where "immigration has always been a central part of nation building". The 2016 Census of Population and Housing revealed that 46% of Australia's 24 million population either were born overseas or have an overseas-born parent. The most common countries of birth, after Australia, were England (5%) and New Zealand (2.5%), but other countries, notably China (2.3%) have become more significant source countries for migrants. Since the mid-2000s, Chinese and Indian arrivals have outpaced arrivals from the United Kingdom and migrants have replaced births as the driver of population growth in Australia (Parliament of Australia, 2010). Further, the 2016 Census shows that over a third (37%) of older people, aged 65 years or over, were born overseas, with the majority born in a non-English-speaking country (Australian Institute of Health and Welfare, 2019). With older overseas-born people who arrived in Australia around the mid-1970s and onwards more likely to have been born in Asia than in Europe (ABS, 2016), the next few decades will see an increasing number of older people of Asian backgrounds in the entire Australian overseas-born population.

This chapter concentrates on Chinese migrants in Australia as the research context, and describes the methodology employed in two studies. The empirical data reported in the next three chapters (Chapters 3–5) were drawn from these two studies. The term "Chinese immigrants" is defined

20 *Research context and methodology*

by the ethnic culture and place of origin, including immigrants who came from mainland China, Taiwan, and Hong Kong. The same definition is commonly applied in defining overseas Chinese in the Euro-American countries (Tan, 2013). The Chinese community in Australia is one of the largest ethnic groups, with more than 1.2 million people who identify as having Chinese ancestry (ABS, 2018). The chapter first provides an overview of Chinese migrants and diaspora in Australia, dating back to the Gold Rush era in the 19th century. These contexts situate the research on how older Chinese migrants build a sense of home in their new country. Building a sense of home is especially significant to Chinese migrants because their culture has a long and strong tradition of family care, with many Chinese preferring to live with their adult children and grandchildren in Australia. Next, the chapter describes the research methodology. Since qualitative research is most appropriate for exploring the meaning of lived experiences of people, the methodology adopted is qualitative in-depth interviews. In one of the two studies, participants not only shared their experiences and stories through individual interviews but also provided photographs that signify home to them. The photo-elicitation method, which accompanied interviews, provides additional depth to interviews as visual elicitation evoked feelings and memories from older Chinese participants and encouraged them to tell their stories. The chapter describes the procedures of participant recruitment, data collection, and data analyses of two studies conducted during 2016–2018 and participated in by 40 overseas-born older Chinese. This chapter highlights that photographs can be a helpful form of visual elicitation for older Chinese participants to voice their experiences in a more engaging way.

Research context

Chinese migration to Australia

In the 18th century, transported criminals were the basis of the first migration to Australia from Europe. Starting in 1788, some 160,000 convicts were shipped to the Australian colonies. Following the initial post-convict settlement, a major impetus for Australian immigration then was the discovery of vast alluvial goldfields. The lure of gold, coupled with the extension of parliamentary democracy and the establishment of inland towns, attracted a mass influx of immigrants in the 1850s. The Gold Rush era of 1851 to 1860 consequently saw early migration peak at arrivals of around 50,000 people a year; with Chinese immigrants comprising the largest non-British group. Approximately 40,000 Chinese labourers arrived in Australia during this period and settled in areas around mining towns in Victoria and other sites

Research context and methodology 21

of labour shortage. The large influx of Chinese labourers caused great concerns among the politicians and miners in Victoria. Some people in the Australian colonies became increasingly worried about the level of "coloured" immigrants, particularly from China, and many colonies subsequently passed restrictive immigration legislation. The *Immigration Restriction Act 1901* was passed by the parliament to limit non-White immigration to Australia, particularly from Asian regions, for the purpose of preserving the predominance of the British immigrant population within Australia. A new feature of the Act was the now infamous Dictation Test, which required the applicant to write out 50 words in any European language selected and dictated by an immigration officer. After 1905, the options available, at the discretion of the immigration officer, expanded to *any* prescribed language. Not surprising, the test became the cornerstone of Australia's White Australia Policy (Jupp, 1988), with a raft of other policies supporting the underlying intention. The colony of Victoria, for example, introduced legislation to discourage Asian immigrants by requesting Chinese arrivals in Victorian ports to pay a £10 head tax. The White Australia Policy reflected Australians' fear of the "Yellow Hordes", as they perceived Asian immigrants, and, indeed, of any immigrants who were not from Britain or northern Europe. This policy was strongly assimilationist, and reflected the belief current at that time that a population must be culturally homogeneous in order to be truly egalitarian and democratic.

The years following the *Immigration Restriction Act 1901* saw a steady decline of the Chinese immigrant population in Australia until the White Australia Policy was removed in 1973 by the then Whitlam Labour Government. The 1970s saw the concept and practice of multiculturalism introduced in Australia, and multiculturalism as a policy was endorsed by the *Racial Discrimination Act* of 1975 (Jupp, 1995). As a result, new waves of Chinese migrants from Hong Kong, Taiwan, and Southeast Asia once again began to arrive on Australian shores. Significant flow of migrants from mainland China began in the 1980s when mainland China began easing restrictions and implemented the "open door" economic policy (Sung & Song, 1991). Many young Chinese took advantage of the changing policy environments in both China and Australia to explore education, career, and business opportunities abroad (Gao, 2017). Between 1995–1996, more than 11,000 mainland China-born migrants had arrived in Australia, accounting for over 11% of the total Australian immigration intake for that year alone (Ip, Lui, & Chui, 2007). The ethnic Chinese population, fewer than 10,000 in the late 1940s, grew steadily to about 50,000 in 1976 and 200,000 in 1986 (Kee, 1992). According to the 2011 Australian Census, around 866,200 Australian residents claimed Chinese origin and as many as 74% were first-generation immigrants (ABS, 2012). Those arrivals between the

22 Research context and methodology

Photo 2.1 Chinatown Melbourne was established in the 1850s for Chinese gold seekers and has been an integral part of Melbourne.

Source: Shuang Liu. Used with permission.

1970s and 1980s, and the parents they brought to Australia after settlement in the country, form a significant proportion of overseas-born older Chinese population in Australia today; the rest were likely those who made their migration journey at a younger age in the 1950s for education, family reunion, business, or other purposes.

Chinese diaspora and Chinatowns

In the context of immigration, diaspora constitutes groups of migrants with strong attachments to their ancestral homeland (Gabriel, 2014) and diaspora community entails the processes by which migrants build a symbolic space

Research context and methodology 23

that links together their country of origin and their country of settlement (Ma, 2003). The Chinese diaspora communities are recognised as the oldest and largest across the world, as well as in Australia (Tan, 2013). For centuries, Chinese diaspora communities have served as social and emotional support for new and old arrivals of Chinese origin, and a source of cultural identification. However, the extent to which Chinese diaspora can choose what identities to assume depends largely on the very delicate balance between them as an ethnic group and the social and political climate in their new country. The pressure for assimilation in those early days of migration to Australia and during the period of White Australia policy created quite a painful experience for many early generations of Chinese migrants. They were required to assimilate to the White dominant Australian society in order to live up to the expectations of Chinese migrants. As a result, some ethnic Chinese felt it necessary to reject their parents' language and culture of their Chineseness; they anglicised their names, dissociated themselves from Chinese relatives and friends, and suppressed their Chinese accent. Some even went to the extent of changing their physical appearances by dyeing their hair and undergoing plastic surgery to appear more "European". However, many of them were still unsuccessful in their efforts to be seamlessly absorbed into the so-called White Australian "melting pot" that they had aspired to (Ha, 1998).

When Chinese migrants moved to the new Australian cultural environment, their cultural and linguistic differences associated with their places of origin became more salient. One typical place of Chinese ethnic distinction is Chinatown. For over two centuries, Chinatowns have been recognised as one of the most visible symbols of overseas Chinese communities across the world. In the second half of the 19th century in Australia, Chinatowns emerged as residential and commercial areas in some cities. The oldest Chinatown in Australia was established in the 1850s in Melbourne for Chinese labourers drawn to Australia during the Gold Rush era to group together and support each other. While Chinatowns can be found in other cities in Australia, Sydney's Chinatown is by far the largest. The origin of Chinatowns owes as much to the segregation by majority groups and colonial governments as they do to the desire of Chinese immigrants to maintain their cultural links to the homeland (Inglis, 2011). The symbolic and physical space was seen as creating pathways for Chinese migrants, particularly early Chinese migrants, to link to their country of origin and, at the same time, to assimilate into the country of settlement. In some previous research on Chinese migrants, scholars have conceptualised such special concentration of ethnic enclaves as ethnoburbs (Zhou & Lin, 2005).

Typically, Chinatowns are characterised by colourful lanterns, restaurants, and Chinese characters on road signs and on shop signs. A typical

24 *Research context and methodology*

feature that tends to characterise Chinatowns across the world is the colourful and ornamental archway, often called dragon gate, which marks the entry to the Chinese space. Similar gates can be seen in Chinese architecture and planning, often as memorial arches incorporated into areas such as palaces or places of historical interest. Archways mark entries to a specific territory; they delineate boundaries, represent a claim to space, and signify permanence as well as visibility. Interestingly, unlike the ancient fortresses in China, the archways in Chinatowns are simply "gates", with no physical walls surrounding Chinatowns. Oftentimes the entry and the exit are not clearly marked, that is, people can go in and go out on different streets or from where they entered. However, a "gate without walls" should not be taken to suggest that Chinatowns do not have spatial limits. Instead, the walls are cultural; they are built by the Chinese language. The distinctive Chinese characters found on shops or on street signs in Chinatowns mark the boundary of a world that stands apart from the rest of the city. Language separates people from people and region from region. Even though the Chinese migrants themselves may speak different dialects, such as Cantonese, Mandarin, Taiwanese or other regional dialects, the Chinese people share the same written language (be it simplified or traditional characters) and Mandarin is considered the standard broadcast language. Through the lenses of architectural distinctiveness, and language and cultural boundaries, Chinatowns serve as a site of Chinese home cultural continuity, community support, and segregation from the large society. For two centuries, Chinese migrants have grouped themselves together for mutual support, and Chinatowns have represented an emblematic space for diaspora community solidarity (Inglis, 2011).

However, the original meaning and significance of Chinatowns as ethnic enclaves has changed in modern days; as our societies become more global, so do our minds. More importantly, the expectations and attitudes to immigrants have changed from assimilation to integration, as a result of change in the immigration policies in many receiving countries, including Australia. Although the multicultural policy in Australia has not eliminated racial discrimination, the original meaning of Chinatowns as a place where the Chinese grouped together for social support and community solidarity has undergone change. The contemporary concept of Chinese diaspora is much broader than it was before, given the Chinese diaspora population now is very heterogeneous and the diasporic space is also much wider. Unlike the their predecessors of the Gold Rush era, who were mostly unskilled labourers from the southern parts of Guangdong Province and Fujian Province in China, the modern-day Chinese immigrant population is much more diverse in terms of education level, skill-bases, socioeconomic status, and occupation. For example, Chinese migrants who arrived in Australia since the 1980s were often well educated, diverse in origin, age, occupation, and socioeconomic status. They include people who were born in different parts of mainland China as well as Taiwan, Hong Kong, and Macau. Their diverse socio-economic backgrounds include highly skilled professionals, well-educated intellectuals, family and spouses, as well as low-skilled workers. Their economic advantage, job skills, and social connections have indicated a break from the settlement patterns established by earlier Chinese migrants.

Consequently, the ethnic enclaves that surrounded Chinatowns have disappeared over time. Chinese settlement after the year 2000 is far more diverse than it has previously been in Australia's metropolitan areas, and new migrants have been presented with numerous settlement options within well-established Chinese communities, including inner-city areas, and often within or adjacent to Chinatown areas or outer suburbs (Wang, Sigler, Liu, & Corcoran, 2018). For example, in Sydney, Melbourne, and Brisbane, Chinese migrants exhibit patterns of deconcentration between 2006 and 2011,

Photo 2.2 Yum cha, involving Chinese tea and dim sum, is a popular Cantonese tradition for family and friends to gather together; the tradition is carried out worldwide where there are overseas Chinese communities.

Source: Shuang Liu. Used with permission.

26 *Research context and methodology*

and inner-city Chinatowns in large Australian cities lost their residential functions and become symbols of cultural and architectural heritage (Wang et al., 2018). Like those in many other parts of the world, Chinatowns in Australia are now tourist attractions as well as shops selling Chinese products including fresh foods, medicinal herbs, and services such as translation agencies or real estate agencies for the Chinese diaspora communities. These changes have led to scholarly debate on the meaning and significance of Chinatowns as a site of diaspora solidarity and identification.

Methodology

The data reported in this book were collected from two studies between 2016 and 2018. Ethical approval for the fieldwork was obtained from the Human Research Ethics Committee of The University of Queensland. A total sample of 40 overseas-born older Chinese immigrants, primarily residing in the city of Brisbane, participated in the studies. Their age ranged from 57 to 86 years. They involved both older Chinese migrants who lived within Chinese ethnic suburbs, and in suburbs lightly populated by people of Chinese origin. The aims of the two studies were to advance an understanding of the processes through which older Chinese migrants attach meaning to home and build a sense of home in Australia. The overarching research questions are these: What does home in a foreign land mean to older Chinese immigrants in Australia? How do they build a sense of home as they age in a foreign land? These research questions are explored in qualitative studies involving in-depth interviews and photo elicitation. This methodology is most appropriate for exploring the meaning of lived experiences of people.

Study 1

The first study was conducted in 2016. Participants ($N = 20$) were recruited using a combination of purposive and snowball sampling strategies. We contacted people of 60 or older with Chinese ancestry at church, community gatherings, informal social activities, and through personal contacts. Eventually, a sample of 20 people agreed to participate in the study, with two participants aged under 60 (56 and 59) and all other participants at the age of 60 and above. The oldest participant was 86 years old and the youngest participant was 56 years old. The two participants under 60 years old were included for two reasons: first, we did not want to drop any participants given the small sample size; and the second reason was that the two participants provided very useful data. Specifically, Participant 1, who was 59 years old at time of the study, moved to Australia at a very young age of 19 years, whereas Participant 20, who was 56 years old at time of

Research context and methodology 27

the study, made the migration journey to Australia at a relatively older age of 41 years. Both of them provided interesting data on the home-building process in Australia.

The sample was approximately gender balanced with 11 females and 9 males. Their length of residence in Australia ranged from 15 to 54 years, with an average length of residence of 31 years. Half of the participants immigrated to Australia when they were under 40 years of age, with the oldest moving to Australia at the age of 60. Before moving to Australia, they worked in a wide range of professions such as accountant, builder, chef, government official, nurse, doctor, office assistant, and technician, and only one person came to Australia as a student. Fourteen participants (70%) reported that the main reason for them to immigrate to Australia was providing their children with a better life and good opportunities for education, whereas the rest (six, 30%) came to Australia for self-education or other reasons. When asked to describe their current roles, most of the participants used the word "grandparents". All of them were born overseas and immigrated to Australia. Although we know that they came from Hong Kong, mainland China, and Taiwan, we could not provide the exact percentage of participants from each place because not all of them specified their place of origin.

A set of semi-structured and open questions were initially presented to all participants in writing, then followed up with face-to-face meetings, conversations over the phone, or on the internet. Open-ended questions allowed the participants to provide descriptions of socially constructed experiences and meanings assigned to real-life experiences, while the semi-structured questions functioned to give them some idea of the focus of the study. The set of questions covered three domains surrounding the two research questions on the meaning of home and home-building in a foreign land. Key questions fell into three categories: (1) the meaning of home and belonging (e.g., What does home mean to you? What are the things that are important to you when you think of your home in Australia, and why? What do you do to build a sense of home in Australia?); (2) cultural identification and intergenerational relationships (e.g., How do you see yourself culturally? Why do you identify culturally the way you do? In what ways do you see your cultural identification similar or different from that of your adult children?); and (3) social connectedness with the community and friend (e.g., What do you do socially? How important do you feel it is to have friends in Australia? How important do you feel to keep connected with old contacts in home country?). Answers to those questions shed light on what the concept of home entails for older Chinese immigrants, what they do to build a sense of home in Australia, and how home is related to their identity and belonging.

28 *Research context and methodology*

I originally planned to interview all participants face to face. However, when we contacted the people who had given consent to participate in the study, almost all of them asked for a written copy of the questions in Chinese characters and indicated that they would like to read them, think through them, and write their answers to those questions at their own pace in their own time. They preferred to go through the questions in a less pressured way, rather than having to answer all questions at one sitting like at face-to-face interviews. Moreover, if they forgot something initially, they could add them when they looked at the questions the second or third time. As a result, we provided a written copy of the questions to all participants, together with pre-paid envelopes for the completed questionnaires to be returned. After providing the questionnaires, we followed up with the participants via the phone and Internet conversations; five participants (25%) approached us to go through the questions and answers with us in what would be like face-to-face interviews. All returned their completed questionnaires. Some answers were written in English; others in Chinese or a mixture of both languages. With the participants' consent, we also digitally recorded the face-to-face conversations with those who had requested the follow-up interviews to go through the questions. Hence, all participants were provided with the same set of questions, although the follow-ups were a mixed mode of phone, face-to-face, and internet. All data collection was conducted in Chinese languages: the written questions provided to the participants were in Chinese characters; the oral communication with the participants was in either Cantonese or Mandarin. Data collection was conducted during February and May 2016.

Study 2

This study also employed a qualitative research approach to explore the meaning of home to older Chinese migrants and their lived experiences of home-building in Australia. Unlike the first study, in Study 2, I asked participants to each provide two photographs signifying home to them, in addition to sharing their experiences and stories through interviews. Previous research using photographs with interviews have examined the social identity of kids, drug addicts, ethnically different immigrants, work worlds, and visual autobiography. In the case of community, photographic studies of identity rely heavily on what is seen, raising the question of what parts of identity are not visible. For example, Gold (1991) used photo-elicitation to explore if and how refugees could visually determine a person's ethnicity and the traits associated with either of the two sub-population. The results showed that the Chinese-Vietnamese and ethnic Vietnamese generally could determine the ethnicity of persons shown and that their categorisation

Research context and methodology 29

of both their own ethnic group and the "other" group were fairly consistent. Another example is a study in which the researchers took photographs of a group of participants while they were doing normal routine activities, followed by interviews asking participants to describe how they interpret the events depicted in the photographs (Snyder & Ammons, 1993). A further example is an earlier study by Van der Does and her four colleagues (1992). They used photo elicitation to explore the cultural definitions of five ethnically distinct Dutch neighbours. The researchers toured the neighbourhood and photographed important topics first. Then they conducted interviews to discover change in the neighbourhood, as perceived by the participants.

In my study, photographs, taken by participants, were considered to be a visualisation of experiences and meanings that the participants assigned to objects, places, and people that were linked to their sense of home in Australia. Scholars in previous studies asked participants to reflect upon the images in interviews or focus groups. For example, Wang and Burris (1997) asked community members to take photographs on a specific theme and conducted focus group discussions afterwards. Of particular relevance to my study is a more recent study using similar method and conducted by van Hees and colleagues (2017), in which photographs were used as data to explore the construction of ageing in place from the perspectives of professionals and older adults. In their study, the researchers asked 18 older adults (aged 75 to 85 years) and 14 professionals (social workers, housing consultants, neighbourhood managers, and community workers) to photograph and discuss the places they consider important for ageing in place. Their findings revealed that ageing in place was associated with specific lived experiences and attachments to specific, intangible, and memory-laden public places for older people and health care professionals. Due to the mobility and logistic constraints, I modified the methods in previous studies by using individual interviews instead of focus group discussions, as used by Wang and Burris (1997). Individual interviews allowed me to devote more time to each individual participant and made the participants feel more relaxed when talking about their ageing experiences in the comfort of their own house, thereby facilitating an in-depth exploration of the nuances of individual experiences. Photographs proved helpful as a form of visual elicitation and a discussion prompt during interviews (Gubrium & Harper, 2013) and, as such, proved an empowering opportunity for my older Chinese participants to voice their experiences in an engaging way.

In terms of participant recruitment, similar to Study 1, I recruited participants through snowball sampling, with the help of one research assistant who is Chinese-English bilingual. We initially contacted potential participants who were in the age range of 55 and above in our social networks

30 *Research context and methodology*

including friends, relatives, and people we met at social events organised by some local Chinese communities. Through a combination of purposive and snowball sampling, we obtained consent from 20 older Chinese to participate in the study. All of the 20 participants were overseas-born Chinese immigrants to Australia, 18 of them moved to Australia from mainland China and two from Hong Kong. The earliest arrival was in 1975 and the most recent was in 2016. Their average length of residence in Australia was around 10 years. The pool of the sample consisted of 13 females (65%) and seven males (35%). Most participants were aged at 60+ (80%), with the youngest being 55 years old and the oldest 83 years old. Most of the participants had retired before they migrated to Australia, and their main purpose for migration was to join their children who made the migration journey before them. This explained the fact that most of the participants had lived or had been living with their children and grandchildren in the same house. When their grandchildren grew up to school age, some of them moved out of their children's house to live independently in a property purchased either by themselves or by their adult children. The circumstances of the two Hong Kong Chinese participants were different, though. They moved to Australia more than three decades ago for the purpose of work. Their children were born and had grown up in Australia. At the time of interview, the two participants were living independently, and not all of their children were in Australia.

The questions for interviews were formulated around the two research questions (What does home mean to older Chinese migrants? and What do they do to build a sense of home as they age in a foreign land?). However, given the use of photo-elicitation method, the interview questions for each participant were around the photographs the participant provided and expanded to a broader discussion on their cultural identity, belonging, and the significance of developing a sense of home in Australia. Example questions include "Can you tell me something about this photo?", "Why do you think this photo conveys to you a feeling of home in Australia?", "What does home mean to you as an older person living in Australia?", and "What kind of things do you do to develop a sense of home in Australia?". Given the nature of the study, not all participants were asked exactly the same set of questions, not just because photographs are different, but also because some interviewees needed more prompts than others. However, in order to ensure the appropriateness of the wording of the main interview questions, we pilot tested the questions with a small group of Chinese; they did not have any problems with responding to the questions.

We collected 40 photographs, some taken by the participants. Although all participants authorised the use of their photos for publication purposes, we re-photographed some of the pictures, objects, and places ourselves,

Research context and methodology 31

partially due to the quality of the originals. All 20 interviews were conducted in the participants' native language (Cantonese or Mandarin) in May 2018. Fourteen interviews (70%) were conducted face to face at the participants' homes in Brisbane. The rest of the participants (six, 30%) were interstate or away from Brisbane at the time of interviewing, and thus their interviews were conducted over the phone or WeChat on the internet (a Chinese multi-purpose messaging, social media, and mobile app). The interviews lasted, on average, one hour each, were digitally recorded, and partially transcribed by the researchers for data analysis.

Data analysis for the two studies

I adopted an inductive thematic analysis technique, which has proven effective in identifying themes that emerge from qualitative data such as interview transcripts where the emphasis is on understanding individual experiences in real-life situations (Boeije, 2002). Thematic analysis was defined by Braun and Clarke (2006, p. 79) as "a method for identifying, analysing, and reporting patterns (themes) within data" and being informed by their framework. Thematic analysis with an inductive approach allowed the themes to emerge from the dataset itself rather than be determined by a specific pre-existing theoretical framework. I conducted the data analysis with the assistance of a research assistant. As both of us are native Chinese speakers, we analysed the data in Chinese. Data analysis was performed in the native language to ensure that the original meaning of the data was retained. Translation from Chinese into English did not occur until we reached the stage of writing up the findings. The reason for not translating the data before analysis was that this strategy would reduce the chance of loss of meaning in the interview data due to translation from Chinese into English.

The analysis process involved iterative steps. The first step was data immersion, which means that the researchers become familiar with the dataset through repeated and thorough reading. The researchers read each completed questionnaire or interview transcript and assigned a code to a sentence, a paragraph, or a section. For example, the code "identity" was assigned to transcripts where issues relating to self-identification as Chinese-Australian were raised. The second step involved the designation of codes based on initial patterns. After data from the first participant was coded, each subsequent reading of the remaining data was carried out in relation to these coded themes identified in the first case. As new themes emerged, new codes were added as necessary. The data were constantly revisited after initial coding, until no new themes were emerging. The third step was to form and refine the themes derived from steps 1 and 2. Once the coding was completed,

32 *Research context and methodology*

the codes that had common elements were merged to form themes. Themes were identified based on repeated patterns of concepts that furthered our knowledge of building a sense of home as they aged in a foreign land. The codes created by the two researchers were compared to ensure consistency of interpretation and to enhance the strength of conclusions drawn from qualitative research. To protect confidentiality, each participant was assigned an identifying number (e.g., 04, 18), and these identifiers were used when extracts were cited in the results chapters (Chapters 3–5).

The same thematic analysis method was used to analyse photographs. The themes and supporting evidence were compared across interviews and photographs, providing illustration of interview data and source of validation and interpretation of interview data. The interviews and photographs complemented each other and enhanced my understanding of the meaning of home and home-building from the perspectives of participants. The findings revealed that photographs provided an opportunity for participants to show why places, objects, and people in the photographs are meaningful, while interviews provided them opportunities to talk about the photographs and explain why those experiences are most significant to them and worthy of sharing. Three key themes were identified surrounding home as a physical place, as a set of relationships, and as a transnational space in-between the old cultural environment they left behind and the new cultural environment they currently live in. These findings will be elaborated in detail in the next three chapters.

Conclusion

This chapter has provided an overview of the history of Chinese migrants and migration to Australia over the past 200 years. The chapter has also described the research methodology used to recruit participants for the two studies, data collection, and data analysis techniques. Chinese migrants form the oldest, largest non-English speaking diaspora communities in Australia. One typical feature of the history of Chinese migrants in Australia is the establishment, function, and change of meaning of Chinatowns. Similar to almost all of the best-known Chinatowns in the world, Chinatowns in Australia were established in the 19th century in response to early Chinese migrants' needs for social support and cultural connection to help them to survive the harsh conditions of the Gold Rush era. Today, Chinatowns are more a space of Chinese cultural representation, attracting tourists and locals, than a source of community solidarity. Although still a place of representation, they are more like cultural icons, images in stories, literature, movies, or on television, than a place of cultural identification for the modern Chinese migrants.

Research context and methodology 33

Because of their size, history, resilience, and cultural significance, Chinese diaspora communities are particularly suited for research on older migrants' search for a sense of home and how they build a sense of home as they live and age in a foreign land. Chinese migrants are more diverse in composition than many ethnic minorities in terms of demographic characteristics, geographic origin, and socio-economic backgrounds. They have spread across more countries under different regimes than other non-White ethnic groups, and historically, have suffered discrimination in more places than most ethnic groups (Benton & Gomez, 2014). Chinese migration in different historical periods served different needs of the country of origin and country of settlement; the migration phenomena should therefore always be examined in the historical contexts. This point is further illustrated by the changing symbolic meaning of Chinatowns. Closely related to the symbolic meaning of Chinatowns in the modern world is the issue of identity. Unlike the forerunners of the Chinese who were under great pressures to assimilate into the larger culture of Australia, particularly during the White Australia policy period, many Chinese migrants in Australia today choose to take root in and identify with both the heritage and host cultures. With advancement in communication technologies, many overseas Chinese maintain close contact with people and events in the home country and their identification as Chinese now is strongly influenced not so much by links with places like Chinatowns or ethnoburbs but, rather, through sources and mediated contacts with their home culture in China, Taiwan, Hong Kong, Macau, or elsewhere. Old imagery of Chinatowns, which encapsulate characteristics of a ghetto as well as a community, a stepping stone to assimilation, is gradually being replaced by Chinatowns as simply a site of cultural diversity in a multicultural society, and a unique cultural symbol standing in a non-Chinese cultural environment.

Despite their relatively large cultural distance from Anglo Australians (e.g., racial characteristics, native language, cultural values, religion, traditions, lifestyle, and so forth), and despite the ordeals that had been faced by generations of Chinese migrants due to stereotypes, prejudice, and racism, many of them have adjusted remarkably well in Australia as their new home. They engage economically, socially, culturally, and politically in their host country while residing abroad but at the same time maintaining close connections with people and events in their home country. For example, Chinese ethnic business entrepreneurs in Australia maintain close ties with their ethnic group because bonds of solidarity within the ethnic community provide resources for business operations as they establish and develop businesses. In addition, ethnic communities may be a source of intangible assets such as values, knowledge, and networks upon which ethnic business people may draw (Liu, 2011). The simultaneous development of a sense of

34 *Research context and methodology*

belonging to the host culture and the maintenance of attachment to the home culture can be a long and challenging process, which involves a mental reconciliation of sometimes incompatible pressures for both assimilation into the mainstream culture and differentiation from it. In the 21st century, however, Chinatowns have taken on new meanings, given the new patterns of migration and the growing influence of China as an economic powerhouse.

The research methodology used here involved a combination of in-depth interviews and photograph elicitation, proved effective in understanding the meaning of home from the perspectives of participants. Images evoke deeper elements of human consciousness than do words (Harper, 2002). Previous research using photographs with interviews to examine Asian immigrants' definition of Asian ethnicity identifies the invisibility of ethnic difference to outsiders (Gold, 1991), through participants' interpretation of events depicted in the photographs taken by researchers (Snyder & Ammons, 1993), and change in ethnically distinctive neighbourhoods as reflected in photographs from the perspectives of participants (Van der Does, Edelaar, Gooskens, Liefting, & van Mierlo, 1992). Common to this previous research is the understanding that photographs add new visual information about our society and people because they induce alternative modes of thought (Pink, 2013). Moreover, using visual information to collect information in research is an opportunity to give voice to unique perspectives, experiences, and meanings. The next chapter illustrates this argument through a detailed discussion of the research findings, particularly related to home as a location and how Chinese migrants build a sense of physical "insideness" as they live and age in Australia.

References

ABS. (2012). Reflecting a nation: Stories from the 2011 census. Retrieved from www.abs.gov.au/AUSSTATS/abs@.nsf/Previousproducts/2071.0Main%20 Features902012–2013?opendocument&tabname=Summary&prodno=2071.0& issue=2012–2013.

ABS. (2016). Ageing population, 2016. Retrieved from www.abs.gove.au/austats/ abs@.nsf/mf/2071.0

ABS. (2018). ABS Chinese New Year insights. Retrieved from http://abs.gov.au/ ausstats/abs%40.nsf/mediareleasesbyCatalogue/D8CAE4F74B82D446CA25823 5000F2BDE?OpenDocument.

Australian Institute of Health and Welfare. (2019). Older Australia at a glance. Retrieved from www.aihw.gov.au/reports/older-people/oder-australia-at-a-glace.

Benton, G., & Gomez, E. T. (2014). Belonging to the nation: Generational change, identity and the Chinese diaspora. *Ethnic and Racial Studies, 37*, 1157–1171.

Boeije, H. (2002). A purposeful approach to the constant comparative method in the analysis of qualitative interviews. *Quality & Quantity, 36*, 391–409.

Research context and methodology 35

Braun, V., & Clarke, V. (2006). Using thematic analysis in psychology. *Qualitative Research in Psychology, 3,* 77–101.

Castles, S. (1992). The Australian model of immigration and multiculturalism: Is it applicable to Europe? *International Immigration Review, 26*(2), 549–567.

Gabriel, S. P. (2014). After the break: Re-conceptualizing ethnicity, national identity and Malaysian-Chinese identities. *Ethnic and Racial Studies, 37,* 1211–1224.

Gao, J. (2017). Rediscovering the new gold mountain Chinese immigration to Australia since the mid-1980s. In M. Zhou (Ed.), *Contemporary Chinese diasporas* (pp. 209–231). Singapore: Palgrave Macmillan.

Gold, S. J. (1991). Ethnic boundaries and ethnic entrepreneurship: A photo-elicitation study. *Visual Sociology, 13*(2), 75–90.

Gubrium, A., & Harper, K. (2013). *Participatory visual and digital methods.* Abingdon and New York: Taylor & Francis.

Ha, M-P. (1998). Cultural identities in the Chinese diaspora. Retrieved from www.arts.uwa.edu.at/MotsPluriels/MP798mph.html.

Harper, D. (2002). Talking about pictures: A case for photo elicitation. *Visual Studies, 17*(1), 13–26.

Inglis, C. (2011). Chinatown Sydney: A window on the Chinese community. *Journal of Chinese Overseas, 7,* 45–68.

Ip, D., Lui, C. W., & Chui, W. H. (2007). Veiled entrapment: A study of social isolation of older Chinese migrants in Brisbane, Queensland. *Ageing & Society, 27,* 719–738.

Jupp, J. (1988). *The Australian people.* Sydney: Angus & Robertson.

Jupp, J. (1995). From "white Australia" to "part of Asia": Recent shifts in Australian immigration policy towards the region. *International Migration Review, 29*(1), 207–228.

Kee, P. K. (1992). The Chinese in Australia: A brief historical overview and contemporary assessment. In Chinese Association of Victoria (Eds.), *Chinese association of Victoria 1982–1992* (pp. 56–76). Melbourne: Chinese Association of Victoria.

Liu, S. (2011). Acting Australians and being Chinese: Integration of ethnic Chinese business people. *International Journal of Intercultural Relations, 35,* 406–415.

Ma, L. J. C. (2003). Space, place and transnationalism in Chinese diaspora. In L. J. C. Ma & C. Cartier (Eds.), *The Chinese diaspora: Space, place, mobility, and identity* (pp. 1–49). New York and Oxford: Rowman & Littlefield.

Parliament of Australia. (2010). *Migration to Australia since federation: A guide to the statistics.* Canberra: Department of Parliamentary Services.

Pink, S. (2013). *Doing visual ethnography.* London: Sage.

Snyder, E. E., & Ammons, R. (1993). Baseball's emotion work: Getting psyched to play. *Qualitative Sociology, 16*(2), 111–132.

Sung, Y., & Song, E. (1991). *The China-Hong Kong connection: The key to China's open door policy.* Cambridge: Cambridge University Press.

Tan, C-B. (2013). Introduction. In C-B. Tan (Ed.), *Routledge handbook of the Chinese diaspora* (pp. 1–12). New York and London: Routledge.

Van der Does, P., Edelaar, S., Gooskens, I., Liefting, M., & van Mierlo, M. (1992). Reading images: A study of a Dutch neighbourhood. *Visual Sociology, 7*(1), 4–67.

36 *Research context and methodology*

van Hees, S., Horstman, K., Jansen, M., & Ruwaard, D. (2017). Photovoicing the neighbourhood: Understanding the situated meaning of intangible places for ageing-in-place. *Health & Place, 48*, 11–19.

Wang, C., & Burris, M. (1997). Photovoice: Concept, methodology, and use for participatory needs assessment. *Health Education & Behaviour, 24*(3), 369–338.

Wang, S., Sigler, T., Liu, Y., & Corcoran, J. (2018). Shifting dynamics of Chinese settlement in Australia: An urban geographic perspective. *Geographical Research, 56*(4), 447–464.

Zhou, M., & Lin, M. (2005). Community transformation and the formation of ethnic capital: Immigrant Chinese communities in the United States. *Journal of Chinese Overseas, 1*(2), 260–284.

3 Home as a place
Physical insideness

Introduction

Gerontology research literature proposes that physical insidedness, defined as a person's familiarity with the physical environment at home and in the neighbourhood where the person lives, is a key component of the person-environment relationship older people maintain in their later life (Rowles, 1983). There are generally two approaches to describing the relationship between older people and their environment: the instrumental approach and the affective approach. The instrumental approach views "home" as a physical space for its residents, "providing shelter and protection for domestic activities and concealment, and an entity separating private from public domains" (Oswald & Wahl, 2005, p. 21). Earlier research on person-environment relations from the instrumental perspective seeks to identify which environmental features are commensurate with the older person's mobility needs and physical competencies, and uses such knowledge to inform how the functioning of some elements in the immediate physical environment could be improved to better suit the older person's needs (Lawton & Nahemow, 1973). The affective approach, on the other hand, is interested in understanding the meanings that older people attach to their experiences with the physical environment at home and in local areas, rather than the functionality of the facilities at home and in local areas (Rowles & Watkins, 2003). Much of the research from the affective approach, therefore, investigates how older people attach meanings to their home as well as to the physical environment in the neighbourhood and local communities.

This chapter adopts the affective approach to explore how older Chinese migrants assign meanings to their home and identifies ways through which attachment to home, neighbourhood, and communities contribute to older Chinese migrants' experience of building a sense of home in Australia. We first provide a critical synthesis of the literature on the relationship among place attachment, place identity, belonging, and well-being. Next, the

38 *Home as a place*

chapter draws on the findings from photographs provided by the participants and in-depth interviews to illustrate how and why the participants believed that familiarity with the physical environment and a sense of control over it are crucial to maintaining their cultural identity continuity and independence in the host country. For example, furniture shipped from the old country and decorations reminiscent of original culture can make participants feel at home in the new country. Moreover, several participants identified backyard gardens as a physical space where the old home in China extends into the new home in Australia. The ability to use public transport to go grocery shopping, meet up with friends at a restaurant, and/or visit a medical practice signifies independence, competence, and a feeling of being at home. Through managing those routines, the participants extend the old self into the new country. The chapter concludes that the development of physical insideness positively contributes to older Chinese migrants' experiences of building a sense of home in Australia and does so through maintaining independence, cultural identity, belonging, and well-being.

Place attachment and place identity

Broadly speaking, place attachment refers to an emotional bond between people and their environments (Brown & Raymond, 2007). Despite the lack of a universal definition of the concept, researchers from different disciplinary areas generally agree on two common dimensions of place attachments: emotional or symbolic attachments, and functional or physical attachments (Lin & Lockwood, 2014). Attachment to a place, be it emotional or physical, is seen as having a key role in building a sense of home among older people, particularly those who moved to a new environment, because such attachment enables them to maintain a sense of continuity of the old self into the new environment (Anton & Lawrence, 2014). Previous research has found that older people tend to report higher levels of place attachment to their homes than to their neighbourhoods (Lewicka, 2010). This could be because the home is a more easily definable space with obvious boundaries, whereas neighbourhoods or local communities are harder to define as they lack obvious boundaries or property lines (Proshansky, Fabian, & Kaminoff, 1983). Moreover, the strength of people's place attachment tends to increase as the amount of contact with a place increases. This supports the argument in the gerontology literature that familiarity with the environment – physical insideness – fosters a sense of identity and belonging in the place an individual resides.

The concept of place identity was first used by Proshansky (1978) who defines it as a type of self-identity consisting of memories, feelings, attitudes, values, preferences, meanings, and all the experience that an individual has with a place. Further, Proshansky et al. (1983) claim that place identity is the product of people's socialisation into the physical world

Home as a place 39

around them, much like an individual's development of a self-identity in a social world, in which one learns to share a commonly shared set of beliefs, values, rules, and norms governing behaviours. In the case of migrants, they undergo cultural transition and relocation from their old country of origin to the new country of settlement. This process of change necessitates the need to develop attachment to the new place of settlement, and rebuild place identity and belonging in the new location that they presently call home. The challenge of rebuilding place attachment and place identity can be even greater for older migrants, particularly those who made their migration journey to a new country at a relatively older age, because they need to deal with the dual challenge of cultural transition over and above that of ageing in a foreign land. Nevertheless, consistent research findings indicate that the development of place attachment and identity can positively contribute to older people's quality of life, physical health, satisfaction with life, social participation, and psychological well-being (Tartaglia, 2012).

Our place identity is not static or fixed. Just as our personal and social identities may change depending on our memberships with different groups at different life stages, place identity is characterised by growth and change in response to changing physical and social environments (Proshansky et al., 1983). For example, Cristoforetti, Gennai, and Rodeschini (2011) explored the changed meanings of home among widows in order to understand the negotiable characteristics of home as a place and place identity. Widowhood is a significant turning point in one's life that can lead to the restructuring of place attachment and identity within the home. In their study, the researchers employed multiple tools as probes for participants to narrate their stories, such as drawings, photographs, a diary, and a suitcase by which the participants bring objects of meaning to interviews. During interviews with the participants, the researchers asked the participants to describe the changes in how spaces at home are used and how the meanings and symbolic connotations embedded in material objects are now renegotiated in light of the changes in their lives brought about by widowhood. The findings identified distinctive processes through which the participants use emotional objects and artefacts to reconstruct the meaning of home, for example, as a place of refuge for the heart and as a place for self-expression. Through identifying the ways in which the participants themselves understand, explicate, and manage daily routines, this study demonstrates that the meaning of home and attachment to home is not fixed, but is subject to negotiation and renegotiation as life circumstances change in older people; the same applies to place identity.

The literature in relation to place attachment and place identity reinforces the notion that home is much more than its physical location and serving functional purposes, rather, home evokes strong social and personal meanings, which can influence the well-being of older people (Sixsmith, 1986). As such, an increasing number of researchers have looked also at the

40 *Home as a place*

emotional and cultural significance of place, and its effect on identity and well-being (Lewin, 2001). For example, a study in the Netherlands found that older migrants place great value on cultural traditions, material objects reminiscent of old culture, and lived experiences in the host country when developing a feeling of belonging (van Hees, Horstman, Jansen & Ruwaard, 2017). Moreover, the concept of home to older people can extend beyond the house to neighbourhoods and communities. For example, findings from another study on the meaning of ageing in place from the perspectives of older people in Australia show that freedom to travel to facilities in local areas by public transport can give older people a sense of place identity and independence (Wiles, Leibing, Guberman, Reeve, & Allen, et al., 2012). Therefore, attachment to place and place identity are cultivated through people's everyday routines, including the use of spaces at home, the emotional significance applied to material objects, and the interactions with the physical environment in the neighbhourhood and local areas (Cristoforetti et al., 2011). As people attribute meanings to their homes and renegotiate them as changes occur in their lives, they become "meaning makers" (Rubinstein, 1990, p. 226). Understanding the meanings of home and the process of home making from the perspectives of older people themselves is critical because the place in which older people live can be a source of either support and opportunity or constraint that affects nearly every aspect of their ageing experiences and outcomes (Wahl & Lang, 2003).

Green spaces signifying home

With most of the participants living in Australia for several decades, attachment to place was identified as a key contributor to a sense of home in Australia: "I have a strong sense of home in where I live [Australia]. I treat my home as permanent residence" (A01, male, aged 59); "I have a very comfortable residence and a living environment. House symbolises home, and home is in the house" (A02, female, aged 61). These expressions showed that migrants' homes are always imbued with the old country and the new country. The meaning "old" home and the "new" home is negotiated within the environment, such as green spaces like private gardens. In one of my studies, several participants showed us photographs of their gardens and talked passionately about how the cultivation of their gardens at home gives them a feeling of home. One participant showed us a photograph of her garden in the backyard and explained,

> This is our backyard. I grow roses and orchid. They are easy to grow. They flower every year. In addition, I grow dessert roses and passionfruit trees. When we look at them every day, they make us feel at home.

Home as a place 41

The first thing we do in the morning after we get up is to go to the garden; we can see the plants when we step out of the house; they give us a very sweet feeling of home.

(B13, female, aged 78)

Another participant expressed a similar sentiment. The housing conditions in her hometown in China did not permit her to grow her own vegetables at home. However, her house in Australia gives her the opportunity to grow

Photo 3.1 Growing Asian vegetables in home gardens communicates a sense of home to older Chinese migrants in Australia.

Source: Siqin Wang. Used with permission.

42   *Home as a place*

vegetables and dragon fruit trees. She described these green spaces as signifying a sense of home to her,

> We grow vegetables and fruit trees in our front yard and backyard. The dragon fruit trees were planted by ourselves, too. Every morning after I get up, I go outside to look at my plants. This is home; it gives me a feeling of home in Australia.
>
> (B08, female, aged 67)

Gardens function to develop a sense of home because those older Chinese can grow plants that remind them of the once familiar environment where they used to live in China. Several participants grow Chinese vegetables, fruit trees, and herbs in their front and backyard. Some participants showed us photographs of the fresh produce they grew such as chilli and flowers they planted such as orchid. Gardens around the house provide a link between the old home and the new home; they are reminiscent of their old self in the home country. In this sense, gardens serve as an extension of the old self into the new country, as well as a means to maintain cultural continuity. Another participant who has grown different kinds of Chinese vegetables in his backyard described how those green spaces remind him of his hometown in China,

> We Chinese like to grow Asian vegetables and fruit trees. I eat the vegetables I grow myself. I also give some of the vegetables I grow to my grandchildren to eat. I used to grow them in my old hometown in the countryside of Wenzhou. But, after we moved to the inner city of Wenzhou and lived in high-rise apartments, it became impossible to grow any vegetables there. Since I'm in Australia now, I can grow them again. My garden reminds me of my old hometown in the countryside of Wenzhou. This gives me a feeling of home.
>
> (B09, male, aged 68)

Similarly, another participant expressed how the plants she grew in her garden function to link her home in China to her home in Australia,

> I grow lots of plants and vegetables in my garden. I also grow lucky bamboos. Every time I look at them, I feel this place is like my hometown. I grow the same kind of lucky bamboos in my hometown in China.
>
> (B20, female, aged 69)

These interview extracts show that gardens represent more than a physical space in the house; rather, they have become an avenue for self-expression

Home as a place 43

and cultural continuity. As the participants cultivate their gardens, they extend their old self from the country of origin to the new environment in the country of settlement. While the gardens' literal roots are in the Australian soil, metaphorically those gardens are embedded in the homeland, and bring memories of the past old location into that of the new and present. These findings demonstrate the role of green spaces in linking migrants' old home in China to their new home in Australia. The memory of the old home in the country of origin is kept alive in the present home in the settlement country through green spaces.

In addition to extending the old hometown into the new Australian context, gardens provide an opportunity for some older Chinese migrants to explore self-potentials, representing the emotional reward that comes from experimenting in the new environment and from developing attachment to the new home. One participant who lived in a high-rise apartment photographed a basket of red peppers she grew on the balcony of her apartment, and she explained,

> I used to live in Shanghai [a large city in China]. I had never grown anything because of space constraints in apartment living over there. It is only after I came to Australia that I began to learn how to grow vegetables on my balcony. My friend introduced gardening to me. I experimented with the tips, and succeeded! I was extremely happy with the results. One day I found some red pepper seeds my friend gave me, I planted them in a pot. Surprisingly, it was a great success [showing the red peppers]. Gardening has become my hobby now; I had never grown anything before coming to Australia; now I am really happy here!
>
> (B02, female, aged 78)

The experience described by this participant revealed that green spaces such as private gardens can build place attachment in older migrants. Through growing plants, caring for them on a daily basis, and reaping the fruits, they develop place attachment and place identity. In the aforementioned example, the green spaces available in her Australian home, contrasted directly with her old home in China, and indicate that Australia provides opportunities that were not available before. In this and many other migrants' experiences, the reward of success in experimenting with gardening techniques enhances satisfaction with life in Australia.

The emphasis on gardens and the outdoors illustrates how external spaces, such as a garden, a balcony or an area outside the house, are lived as internal spaces to build a sense of home. Cristoforetti and colleagues (2011) used the expression "the introjection of external spaces" to describe the process whereby a non-domestic space outside the house is transformed

44 *Home as a place*

into a domestic one, bringing the outside into the home. In their study on the renegotiation of the meaning of home for widows, they found that older participants established strong emotional relationships not only with the plants and flowers that they cared for, but also with all the natural elements with which they came into contact. Much of the existing literature in gerontology explores the role of green spaces in nursing homes or retirement villages. For example, Raske (2010) found that gardens play an immensely positive role in the lives of older adults who live in nursing homes, particularly for those with dementia. For these residents, the garden is a place for meaningful activities, an opportunity to connect with other residents, and greater satisfaction with life. There is little research, however, that explores the social and cultural significance of private gardens in creating a sense of home, particularly for migrants who face the challenge of rebuilding home in a foreign land. Since the findings from our studies suggest that gardens play an important role for older Chinese migrants to link their old home in the homeland to their new home in a foreign land, future research may explore further the social and cultural roles of gardens in improving older people's ageing experiences. Knowledge generated from such research can add a new dimension to understandings of the meanings of home and home-making from the perspective of older migrants themselves.

In addition to gardens, public spaces outside of the home, such as parks, restaurants, beaches, oceans, and places for gathering together and participating in social activities such as school or community halls, may play a significant role in making people feel at home in the new country. For example, there is hardly a shopping centre, big or small, in Brisbane, Australia, that is without a Chinese restaurant. However, these restaurants are not simply places that provide authentic Asian or Chinese cuisine. More importantly, they represent a culture icon and social place where Chinese migrants gather together with family and friends. Seven participants showed us photographs taken with their friends at such outings or gatherings to highlight the importance of maintaining social networks to older people's well-being. A participant who has lived in Australia for 14 years showed us a picture of him with a group of older Chinese in a Chinese restaurant, to express how such gathering gives him a sense of home in Australia,

> This photograph was taken in a restaurant where we catch up with a regular group of friends. We have similar backgrounds and enjoy talking with each other. I used to live in a non-Chinese suburb; I did not have friends and often stayed at home, feeling isolated. Later, I moved to Sunnybank area [a place characterised by concentration of Chinese

Home as a place   45

residents, shops, and services], it became much better. To catch up with such a group of friends gives me a feeling of home in Australia.

(B14, male, aged 83)

Our findings on the cultural significance of public places are echoed in other studies that revealed parks, benches and outdoor seating areas can be important to the health and well-being of older people by providing places for them to connect with others socially (Ottoni, Sims-Gould, Winters, Heijnen, & McKay, 2016). Similarly, the study by Coleman and Kearns (2015) explored how older people engaged with blue spaces in Waiheke Island in New Zealand as therapeutic landscapes, and found that blue oceans can function as a symbolic connection with the past and present and self, as well as a resource of independence in the lives of older people. Even watching others enjoying the surf or the sand at the beach can have a calming effect on people coping with challenging situations. This finding is of particular relevance in context of this study because southeast Queensland is well known for its warm, subtropical climate, and its stunning beaches. Similar to gardens, familiarity with public places such as beaches, restaurants, and parks and the ability to engage with them can create a sense of home for older migrants.

Almost all participants mentioned friendly Australian people, well-developed health care system, freedom to practise and maintain heritage cultural traditions, good social security, fresh air, beautiful natural environment, and quality of life as reasons for their feeling at home in Australia. Those findings support the literature that the concept of home extends into neighbourhood, local communities, even into the larger social, political, and cultural environment of the country, reinforcing the importance of place and people in cultivating a sense of home. The desire to keep close to Chinese co-ethnics led to most participants living in suburbs densely populated by residents of Chinese heritage, and in residential areas close to Chinese or Asian services, such as restaurants, Chinese traditional medicine practices, Asian groceries stores, Asian hairdressers, travel agencies, and Chinese community associations, to mention just a few. Ethnic enclaves give migrant residents a sense of home beyond the house and make life more convenient for those who do not speak fluent English; furthermore, the social engagement with co-ethnics facilitated by such areas can reduce isolation as friendship networks provide a sense of home in a foreign land. Being close to ethnic services and residing in a Chinese ethnic enclave facilitate social participation, mobility, and independence.

The physical insideness with a place that older people develop over time leads to the place becoming an extension of the self (Rowles, 1993). Simple things such as learning to get out and about by bus can instil a feeling of independence and confidence that migrants once had as their old self in the old country. However, in the new country, those habits and activities that provide a sense of self-assurance and self-reliance often need to be relearned. For example, in China, buses stop at every bus stop, whereas, in Australia they only do so at passengers' request, usually made by pressing a button to alert the driver. This difference is one that could be initially disorienting and stressful for an elderly migrant who is not used to this procedure, and one that would have to be relearned in order to do it successfully. Social engagement with co-ethnics and independence in navigating daily routines, for example, going to a local grocery store, and meeting up with friends in a restaurant, help to build a sense of home in Australia. Research shows that people who have a strong place attachment and identity to local areas are more likely to be socially active by joining clubs and community associations and involving in local volunteer activities (Cuba & Hummon, 1993). Place attachment, therefore, can influence the extent to which older people get involved in their local communities.

Photo 3.2 Bus stations represent links between home and the outside world; the ability to get out and about by bus gives older Chinese migrants a feeling of being at home in Australia.

Source: Shuang Liu. Used with permission.

Home as a place 47

Material objects signifying home

Material objects were also featured prominently within the study, often as symbols that bridge the distance between the "old" and the "new" home. While green spaces such as private gardens provide a space for older Chinese migrants to extend their old self into the new cultural environment, material objects embedded with emotional and cultural significance play a key role in creating a sense of home for older Chinese. Many older Chinese in Australia prefer to live with their adult children and grandchildren, although the number of Chinese migrants living independently is on the increase in recent years. Regardless of differences in views on familial living arrangements, migrants' sense of home and belonging always straddles across homeland to the foreign land, albeit to a different extent. This is particularly the case for those who have relatives such as parents that are still alive in China. For elderly Chinese migrants, the sense of belonging to China is especially strong if their children still live there. For example, one participant who migrated to Australia about four years ago described her belonging to home country and host country as,

> Half of my belonging goes to Australian home and the other half to my China home because my daughter is here and my son is in China. It is good to live here with my daughter, and it is equally good to live with my son in China. So my home is in two places; it's how I link Australia with China. Blood ties are important.
>
> (B20, female, aged 69)

Furthermore, belonging increases when there is a sense of grounding. For several participants – even relatively recent arrivals – this sense of grounding came from owning a property. One participant who moved to Australia three years ago when her daughter began to pursue higher education in Australia told us,

> In terms of belonging, I'd give 30% to my home in Australia and 70% to my home in my hometown in China. As I live here longer, my feeling of belonging has increased. What gave me a sense of grounding is that I bought the house; the house means that I have a place of our own to live in [meaning they did not have to rent a place to live anymore].
>
> (B01, female, aged 60)

Similar feelings were expressed by a long-term migrant, who described how property ownership could translate into a strong feeling of place attachment,

> When I migrated to Australia more than 30 years ago, I lived in the Gold Coast. I moved home several times [because of renting], but all

48 *Home as a place*

in the Gold Coast area. It is after we bought this house, I began to feel settled down. I no longer need others to offer accommodation to me. This is my own free space; this is my own home.

(B05, male, aged 71)

Property ownership provides migrants with a sense of grounding, and it in turn, makes them feel "at home". However, at the same time, they are aware that their "home" is also situated in a foreign land. To make their Australian house a home of their own, many participants used decorations, furniture, or paintings to add Chineseness to their home. Several participants used material objects to prominently feature their Chinese identity, bridging the distance between the old and the new home. They decorated their house with artefacts, furniture, and paintings reminiscent of Chinese culture to remind them of their home in the home country, and to create a sense of cultural continuity. Some of the quotes included, "There is a feeling of home because I can look at familiar furniture and photos" (A20, female, aged 56); "I designed the house and decorations which all have Chinese cultural elements in them to make it feel like home" (A13, male, aged 65); and "I have Chinese items on display as decoration of my house to make it a Chinese home" (A12, female, aged 63).

This connection between the "old" and the "new" home is represented in one participant's photograph of her study room. She migrated to Australia in the year of 2014 to join her daughter's family. During the interview, she showed us her study, which is filled with objects and furniture embedded with emotional and cultural meanings. The participant explained,

This is my study in the house. There are tea sets and bookcases. I painted the lotus picture myself. I came from Jinan, Shandong Province. The painting features a lotus of Da Ming Lake – an icon of my hometown. All of the decorations and furniture in this room were shipped to here from my hometown in China. Our house [she lived with her daughter's family] is decorated the American style, but I made my study very Chinese style. You would feel as if you were in China the moment you walk into this room. This study always reminds me of my Chinese cultural roots and it reflects my nostalgic feeling for my hometown in China. My daughter's foreign friends like my study, too, when they visit our house.

(B07, female, aged 60)

The objects and furniture in the study are special to the participant because they were brought to Australia from her hometown, and they therefore link the old country of origin with the new country of settlement. Whenever

Home as a place 49

she looks at these objects in her house in Australia, she is reminded of her homeland and cultural roots. In so doing, she feels connected to home in both places. These objects provide a daily opportunity for the participant to (re)create the "old" home through memories, and connect to her culture, and family. This suggests that the memory of culture can be kept alive through physical objects. Through this lens, the participant's cherished cultural objects which can be understood as a physical representation of the past, the present, and possibly the future. The importance of meaningful objects reinforces an understanding of home as a "a warehouse of memories, connecting past and present self" (Stones & Gullifer, 2016, p. 458), rather than simply as a place of refuge or shelter, and corroborates a recent study by Liu (2015), which found that physical objects and cultural practices can have significant cultural and emotional meanings to immigrants as they search for a sense of home in Australia. Moreover, in addition to the emotional significance older migrants attach to those culturally embedded objects and artefacts, those material objects also allow us to see what they enable people to do with them, in other words, how objects and people co-construct the meaning of home.

The link between the old and the new cultures represented by material objects also serve to provide a sense of cultural identity continuity among older Chinese because they see home as a place where they can preserve and continue their Chinese cultural identity, in their words, their home is where they feel as a Chinese in Australia. Material objects become an important component of the sense of self because they are incorporated into the extended cultural self (Cristoforetti et al., 2011). One participant embroidered traditional Chinese arts on pieces of cloth, framed them and put them up on the wall (B11, female, aged 65). Still, another participant has Chinese couplets and Chinese calligraphy by a famous Chinese calligrapher on the wall (B14, male, aged 83) because those objects have emotional attachment and extend Chinese culture into their new home in Australia. When it is traditional festival season, they often put up decorations outside the house to signify that their home is a Chinese home in Australia, as this participant told us,

> During the Chinese New Year, we will hang lanterns and fish-shaped cloth decorations to symbolise that there is always more than enough to eat and spend in the house every year (*nian nian you yu*).
>
> (B10, female, aged 55)

Even when celebrating Western festivals such as Christmas, some Chinese food can be found on the dining table. One participant presented a photograph taken at one Christmas dinner at home. In the photograph, although

50 *Home as a place*

the dining table was decorated with Christmas decorations in the Western style, a bowl of lychee (a type of Chinese fruit) was on the table, served by itself, not as accompaniment for a dish, as is usually the case in Western dishes.

> We are Australian Chinese because we have lived here for a long time, but still Chinese because we speak Mandarin. I have a big picture of rose, drawn by my old classmate. In addition, I have Chinese calligraphy and backyard garden – they all give me a sense of home here.
>
> (B13, female, aged 78)

These findings showed that the element of Chineseness is in all participants' cultural identification, and this has not changed even for those who have resided in Australia for over 40 years and have since become an Australian citizen. Even those long-term migrants who immigrated to Australia when they were about 20 years of age and are fluent in English view Chinese as an important part of their identity, seeing themselves as Australian-Chinese, instead of only Australian, or only Chinese.

Interestingly, visits by friends from the home country can strengthen migrants' sense of home in Australia, as well as remind them of their own ties with the home country. One participant showed us a photograph she took with friends from her hometown when they visited her in Australia. She then explained,

> This photograph was taken with two friends on the balcony of my apartment. They are my friends from China. When they came to Australia for sightseeing, they visited me and stayed in my apartment for a week. This experience shows that my friends recognise that my home is in Australia. If I had not settled down in Australia, they would not have come to visit me. It made me feel that I have an Australian home.
>
> (20, female, aged 69)

The empirical data from our studies illustrate that the notion of home is a fluid and multifaceted concept. There is a constant negotiation between the old and the new home, through stories, memories, material objects, and relationships. Despite some participants having lived in Australia for decades, all recognised the Chinese component in their cultural identity, and that Chineseness does diminish with time. For migrants, home in the new country is always a place where traditional culture is continued in the host country. Such cultural continuity can be achieved through decorating the house with cultural objects and furniture, and designing gardens to reflect Chinese culture or to be reminiscent of life in the hometown. These

Home as a place 51

findings reinforce the acculturation literature that migrants do not make a sharp break with their homeland upon migrating to a new country, and that, instead, they continuously bridge the two places by extending their old self into the new cultural context.

Conclusion

This chapter explores the meaning of home as a place, and how older Chinese migrants build their sense of home through developing place attachment to home, neighbourhood, and communities and place identity, or in Rowles' (1983) words, physical insideness. Taking an affective approach and drawing on the findings from photographs and interviews, this chapter illustrates the processes older Chinese undergo to make their environment familiar to them, and the means they employed to maintain their cultural identity continuity and independence in the host country. The research findings show that green space such as the gardens migrants create in their own home represent more than a physical place; rather, it represents the emotional feeling of having one's own place and the freedom to cultivate the self through the growing of fruits, vegetables, and plants, even bringing memories of the past into the present home. Moreover, the findings from my research support the literature on the importance of cultural objects as a means to bridge the distance between the old home and the new home to maintain a sense of cultural identity (Zhan, Wang, Fawcett, & Fan, 2017). As a migrant's home in the host country is always associated with both home country and host country, cultural objects help to continue the old self into the host country. Further, the findings from my research demonstrates that the ability to use public facilities and services, such as restaurants, parks, and buses, can positively contribute to building independence, confidence, place attachment, place identity, belonging, and a sense of home in the once unfamiliar environment in the host country. The chapter concludes that the development of physical insideness positively contributes to older Chinese migrants' experiences of building a sense of home in Australia through maintaining independence, cultural identity, belonging, and well-being.

That environmental gerontology involves "the description, explanation, and modification or optimization of the relation between the elderly person and his or her environment" (Wahl & Weisman, 2003, p. 616) has remained salient. What has changed in the theoretical application in more recent years is an increased emphasis on the meaningful content of person-environment transactions, often embodied in the terms "place" and "home". Van Hees and colleagues (2017) identified four types of places. The first is the home, the second is the workplace, the third includes public and community spaces, and the fourth is a place of the past that is kept alive by

52   *Home as a place*

memories, stories and communication. This fourth place, albeit intangible, functions as a significant resource for ageing in a foreign land because it enables older migrants to maintain an emotional connection to their homeland and culture. The relationship between older people and their physical environments is not fixed (Cutchin, 2013), rather it involves a lifelong process of integration and reintegration of people and place, shaped by changes in both individuals and environments. Over time people form attachments to the settings of everyday life. In selecting, furnishing, modifying and personalising these environments, they make a place a home (Cutchin, 2004) and make themselves at home (Wahl & Lang, 2003).

Consistent research shows that older people prefer to age in place (Luborsky, Lysack, & van Nuil, 2011). For example, the Australian Government's policy settings around aged care emphasise the importance of older Australians ageing in place: to live independently and comfortably in their own homes and local communities for as long as possible. In addition to the benefits of familiarity with the environment, the comfort of being in one's own home, and closer contact with family and friends, ageing in place allows older people to continue to contribute to the social fabric of their families and local communities, and also receive the services, care, and support they need when required. Previous research has shown that place attachment influences the extent to which older people get involved in their local communities (Rubinstein, 1990), such as joining clubs, participating in volunteer activities in the communities and engaging in socially connecting with others who are similarly attached to the same place (Cuba & Hummon, 1993). Immigrants face greater challenges in rebuilding place attachment and place identity in the new country because many once familiar routines would need to be relearned, for example using public transport. Moreover, there is a need for them to maintain cultural identity continuity and extend the old self into the new country through engaging in those activities. The next chapter discusses how cultural identity continuity is maintained through family and social relationships.

References

Anton, C. E., & Lawrence, C. (2014). Home is where the heart is: The effect of place of residence on place attachment and community participant. *Journal of Environmental Psychology, 40,* 451–461.

Brown, G., & Raymond, C. (2007). The relationship between place attachment and landscape values: Towards mapping place attachment. *Applied Geography, 27,* 89–111.

Coleman, T., & Kearns, R. (2015). The role of blue spaces in experiencing place, aging and wellbeing: Insights from Waiheke Island, New Zealand. *Health & Place, 35,* 206–217.

Home as a place 53

Cristoforetti, A., Gennai, F., & Rodeschini, G. (2011). Home sweet home: The emotional construction of places. *Journal of Aging Studies*, *25*, 225–232.

Cuba, L., & Hummon, D. M. (1993). A place to call home: Identification with dwelling, community and region. *The Sociological Quarterly*, *34*, 111–131.

Cutchin, M. P. (2004). Using Deweyan philosophy to rename and reframe adaptation-to-environment. *The American Journal of Occupational Therapy*, *58*, 303–312.

Cutchin, M. P. (2013). The complex process of becoming at-home in assisted living. In G. D. Rowles & M. Bernard (Eds.), *Environmental gerontology: Making meaningful place in old age* (pp. 105–123). New York, NY: Springer.

Lawton, M. P., & Nehemow, L. (1973). Ecology and the ageing process. In C. Eisdorfer & M. P. Lawton (Eds.), *Psychology of adult development and aging* (pp. 619–674). Washington, DC: American Psychological Association.

Lewicka, M. (2010). What makes neighbourhood different from home and city? Effects of place scale on place attachment. *Journal of Environmental Psychology*, *30*, 35–51.

Lewin, F. A. (2001). The meaning of home among elderly immigrants: Directions for future research and theoretical development. *Housing Studies*, *16*(3), 353–370.

Lin, C., & Lockwood, M. (2014). Forms and sources of place attachment: Evidence from two protected areas. *Geoforum*, *53*, 74–81.

Liu, S. (2015). Searching for a sense of place: Identity negotiation of Chinese immigrants. *International Journal of Intercultural Relations*, *46*, 26–35.

Luborsky, M. R., Lysack, C. L., & van Nuil, J. (2011). Refashioning one's place in time: Stories of household downsizing in later life. *Journal of Aging Studies*, *25*, 243–252.

Oswald, F., & Wahl, H. W. (2005). Dimensions of the meaning of home in later life. In G. D. Rowles & H. Chaudhury (Eds.), *Home and identity in late life: International perspectives* (pp. 21–45). New York, NY: Springer.

Ottoni, C. A., Sims-Gould, J., Winters, M., Heijnen, M., & McKay, H. A. (2016). "Benches become like porches": Built and social environment influences on older adults' experiences of mobility and well-being. *Social Sciences & Medicine*, *169*, 33–41.

Proshansky, H. M. (1978). The city and self-identity. *Environment and Behavior*, *10*, 147–169.

Proshansky, H. M., Fabian, A. K., & Kaminoff, R. (1983). Place-identity: Physical world socialization of the self. *Journal of Environmental Psychology*, *3*, 57–83.

Raske, M. (2010). Nursing home quality of life: Study of an enabling garden. *Journal of Gerontological Social Work*, *53*(4), 336–351.

Rowles, G. D. (1983). Place and personal identity in old age: Observations from Appalachia. *Journal of Environmental Psychology*, *3*, 299–313.

Rowles, G. D. (1993). Evolving images of place in aging and "aging in place". *Generations*, *17*, 65–70.

Rowles, G. D., & Watkins, J. F. (2003). History, habit, heart, and hearth: On making spaces into places. In K. W. Schaie, H-W. Wahl, J. Mollenkopf, & F. Oswald (Eds.), *Aging independently: Living arrangement and mobility* (pp. 77–96). New York, NY: Springer.

54 *Home as a place*

Rubinstein, R. L. (1990). Personal identity and environmental meaning in later life. *Journal of Aging Studies, 4*(2), 131–147.

Sixsmith, J. A. (1986). The meaning of home: An exploratory study in environmental experience. *Journal of Environmental Psychology, 6,* 281–298.

Stones, D., & Gullifer, J. (2016). "At home it's just so much easier to be yourself": Older adults' perceptions of ageing in place. *Ageing & Society, 36,* 449–481.

Tartaglia, S. (2012). Different predictions of quality of life in urban environments. *Social Indicators Research, 113*(3), 1045–1053.

van Hees, S., Horstman, K., Jansen, M., & Ruwaard, D. (2017). Photovoicing the neighbourhood: Understanding the situated meaning of intangible places for ageing-in-place. *Health & Place, 48,* 11–19.

Wahl, H. W., & Lang, F. R. (2003). Aging in context across the adult life course: Integrating physical and social environmental research perspectives. In H. W. Wahl, R. J. Scheidt, & P. G. Windley (Eds.), *Annual review of gerontology and geriatrics* (pp. 1–33). New York, NY: Springer.

Wahl, H. W., & Weisman, G. D. (2003). Environmental gerontology at the beginning of the new millennium: Reflections on its historical, empirical and theoretical development. *The Gerontologist, 43*(5), 616–627.

Wiles, J. L., Leibing, A., Guberman, N., Reeve, J., & Allen, R. E. S. (2012). The meaning of "ageing in place" to older people. *The Gerontologist, 52*(3), 357–366.

Zhan, H. J., Wang, Q., Fawcett, Z., Li, X., & Fan, X. (2017). Finding a sense of home across the Pacific in old age: Chinese American Senior's report of life satisfaction in a foreign land. *Journal of Cross-Cultural Gerontology, 32,* 31–55.

4 Home as relationships
Social and cultural insideness

Introduction

To understand home as a set of relationships for older Chinese migrants, we can start with the pictographic Chinese character of home (家), which is comprised of two parts: a roof at the top and pigs at the bottom under the roof. There are different speculations about why the Chinese character of home depicts pigs in a house rather than a person. One explanation relates to the practice of animal husbandry. Because pigs are domesticated animals, a house with a pig in it inevitably means that it is a house for people, too. Another explanation is that pigs are commonly used as a sacrifice to one's ancestors, especially during Chinese New Year celebrations. Therefore, pigs symbolise respect for familial ancestors. Still other explanations include that, in ancient China, the livelihood of a family could not be sustained by relying simply on hunting. Many people raised pigs as food in times of famine; hence a house with pigs became the symbol of family. In the eyes of ancient Chinese, a shelter was not a true home unless it had pigs in it. Only a house with pigs could be considered as a self-sufficient home with a secure livelihood. What these different explanations have in common is that the domestication of animals played a key role in the making of home that allowed family members to live under the same roof in ancient China. While we might not be able to verify which or if any of the origin explanations are true, the stories still reveal the fundamental assumption underlying what constitutes a Chinese home – family members living under the same roof. This original meaning of the Chinese home, dating back to ancient times, has evolved in modern days to include the emotional aspect of place attachment, identity, belonging, and the social and cultural dimensions of roles and responsibilities of family members, in addition to home as a physical place.

This chapter explores the concept of home as a set of relationships, primarily family and social. The chapter first discusses family relationships, in

56 *Home as relationships*

particular intergenerational relationships, in Chinese families in Australia. It is common to see older Chinese migrants live in the same house as their adult children and, oftentimes, grandchildren. In this arrangement, traditional Chinese families follow the Confucian tradition of differentiated roles, responsibilities, and obligations of parents, children, wives and husbands, and brothers and sisters. However, generational differences in adherence to traditional cultural values and practices can lead to conflict in intergenerational relationships. For example, filial piety, the virtue and primary duty of respect, obedience, and care for one's parents and elderly family members, is treasured among older Chinese migrants; many of them expect to live with their adult children and to be cared for by the younger generation. Yet, in Australia and many other Western countries, this is not the cultural norm expected of adult children, who may have acculturated faster than the older generation. Instead, they tend to see filial piety more in terms of the provision of financial support to elderly parents. The awareness of generational differences, in a way, made older Chinese more aware of the importance of developing new social networks with friends and neighbours in the host country because the opportunity to share cultural practices (such as recipes) and even personal experiences (such as intergenerational conflicts) is emotionally comforting. Drawing on data from the empirical studies we conducted, this chapter illustrates how older Chinese migrants build a sense of home in Australia through maintaining family and social relationships, and it demonstrates how the social and cultural aspects of home give them a sense of identity and belonging in Australia. It is through intergenerational relationships, social networks, and participation in community activities that older Chinese migrants develop social and cultural insidedness, which refers to a person's integration into the social and cultural environment through everyday interactions with people and the environment.

Family and social relationships

Connections with family and social networks play a significant role in enhancing the quality of life for older people and psychological well-being because such connections give them a purpose and meaning in life and a link to the outside world (Register & Herman, 2010). Earlier studies on older Asian migrants in the United States found that they were more likely to reside in extended family households, be cared for by family members, and to contribute in various ways to the family on which they rely for social and material support (Treas & Mazumdar, 2002). Such practice has continued to the present day in many Asian migrant families in immigrant-receiving countries like Australia. Many Chinese migrants, particularly those who made their migration journey at a relatively older age, moved to the new

Home as relationships 57

country to join their children who had settled down there before them. In countries like Australia, they are most likely to have arrived on a sponsored parent visa. A basic requirement for this type of visa is that adult children support their parents practically and financially for the first few years following their arrival, before they can be considered eligible for government support (Department of Home Affairs, 2019). Hence, the quality of intergeneration relationships plays a significant role in either decreasing or increasing older parents' feeling of home in the host country in which they live.

A fundamental Chinese value is the importance of the family unit. In contrast to the emphasis placed on individuals in most Western societies, Chinese regard the family, not the individual, as the basic social unit (Ward & Lin, 2010). Every Chinese from an early age learns to think of family first and strive to maintain close and harmonious family relations (Hwang, 1999). The Chinese people believe in the importance of supporting and assisting the family in ways such as helping siblings and relatives, looking after parents, and by extension helping the friends of family members when needed. Such emotional attachment and faithfulness to the family are viewed as a duty, not a choice, and such sense of responsibility is engrained in the core of Chinese identity (Ward & Lin, 2010).

In a traditional extended Chinese family, Confucian norms of elder care and deference to the elderly parents are observed (Lin, Bryant, Boldero, & Dow, 2015). Filial piety, a central family value to Chinese, can be defined as the expression of responsibility, respect, sacrifices, and family harmony that regulates children's attitudes and behaviour towards elderly parents (Wong, Yoo, & Stewart, 2006). Children in traditional Chinese families are raised to respect their parents and are socialised to care for them as they age. Filial children, especially the eldest son, are expected to sacrifice their own interest for the well-being of their elderly parents. Adolescents who show loyalty to the family by maintaining good relationships with family members and fulfilling family responsibilities are perceived by Chinese parents as ideal children because filial piety encompasses qualities of respect, commitment, and obligations to one's family (Ketrow & DiCioccio, 2009).

Although filial piety continues to influence older parent-child relationship in Chinese families, many older Chinese migrants have adjusted their filial expectations in the host country (Ip, Lui, & Chui, 2007). They are aware of generational differences in adherence to traditional cultural practices. They also recognise that they themselves need to adjust to the host culture that is more oriented towards individualism than the collectivistic culture they came from. In adjusting and changing in expectations, many older Chinese migrants place increasing emphasis on independence, autonomy, and self-reliance (Lin et al., 2015). For example, they may choose to live in separate houses from their adult children, when such option is available to them, and

58 *Home as relationships*

they place value on being both physically and financially independent from their children when they can. However, they still prefer to live close to their adult children and grandchildren so that family members can easily help each other when needed and gather together at weekends or during holidays. Therefore, while living in the host country can initiate adjustments in expectations around the ways in which filial responsibility is played out between the generations, blood ties and good intergenerational relationships still remain very important in Chinese families.

In many ways, the very awareness of generational differences encourages older Chinese to rebuild their social networks through which they can connect with others who are of a similar ethnic background, are of a similar age, and have a similar migration experiences. Older people are at greater risk of isolation and loneliness due to the many life changes that might take place in later life, including retirement, bereavement, and children and friends moving away. Social relationships are found to be an important predictor of well-being across the life course, but may be particularly salient for older people (Park, Morgan, Wiles, & Gott, 2019). For example, participation in social activities such as going on day trips with friends, gathering with friends at a restaurant, or visiting a friend's house are perceived as important for the well-being of older people. Social relationships include multiple dimensions such as the size of individuals' social networks, frequency of contact with people within the network, and engagement in social activities (Shankar, Rafnsson, & Steptoe, 2015). Studies have showed that a greater number of daily interactions with others, even those who were not close network members was associated with higher levels well-being (Sandstrom & Dunn, 2014).

Developing new social network ties is especially critical for older migrant populations because research shows that older migrants are at elevated risk of social isolation due to loss of cultural and social connections (Park & Kim, 2013). When cultural transition occurs, migrants lose valued relationships with people from their country of origin and face the challenge of rebuilding social networks in their country of settlement. Consistent research in the field of ageing has identified social isolation among migrants to be correlated with loneliness (Ip et al., 2007), reduced satisfaction in life, and low psychological well-being (Meijering & Lager, 2014), For this group, any loss of connectedness can undermine their ability to socially engage in the host society, thereby hindering their capacity to age well in a foreign land. Moreover, social isolation is not just experienced by new arrivals (those within the first six months of immigration), but also amongst older migrants who have lived in the settlement country for decades. Like new arrivals, this latter group can also face difficulties with a loss in social connectedness particularly when compared with their older non-migrant counterparts, such as problems in rebuilding social networks that can be caused by language barriers (Zhan et al., 2017).

Home as relationships 59

Social networks provide migrants with a sense of social location and belonging (Yuval-Davis, 2010) as well as a source of social support. Such a sense of location and belonging, in turn, develops identity, which expresses an individual's emotional attachment to the place they presently call home. Scholars recognise that a reduction in social connectedness among older people is often related to their reduced engagement with the local environment (Hodge, English, Giles, & Flicker, 2013). This is particularly the case for old migrants who have more obstacles to connect to the host society than their non-migrant counterparts, due to unfamiliarity with the local environment, and in some cases, due to relatively a small number of co-ethnics or ethnic services in the local area (Li & Chong, 2012). As such, even those older migrants who have relatively good health and mobility might be afraid to go outside the house due to low English language proficiency and unfamiliarity with the local environment. They may have to rely on their children for providing transportation if they do not know how to drive or how to access public transport, communicate with drivers, or if they live in suburbs beyond walking distance to public facilities such as bus stations, medical providers, restaurants, and shopping centres. This shows that while social connectedness describes how people relate with friends and social groups, it requires older people's ability to navigate the physical environment where they live in order to access the facilities, social networks, and other support services (Wahl & Oswald, 2010). The social and the physical are therefore intertwined and self-perpetuating – increased physical connectedness can encourage participation in social activities, enhanced levels of social engagement can, in turn, increase a person's desire and ability to confidently navigate the physical environment to access available social support and services, thereby building and reinforcing social networks. Ageing well in a foreign land is not just about developing attachment to a particular home. More importantly, it involves an older migrant's capacity to continually reintegrate with place and people in the host country.

While a number of studies have investigated the importance of family and social relationships to older people's perceived quality of life and well-being, a less researched area is the role of social relationships with neighbours in creating a sense of belonging to the community (Gardner, 2011). Although family has been identified as the most important source of support among older people, there is increasing awareness of the important role played by non-family support, in particular, the role of friends and neighbours in enhancing well-being for older adults (Walker & Hiller, 2007). Gardner (2011, p. 266) proposed the term "third places" to refer to public places located outside the home (first place) and work (second place), and local areas such as sidewalks in the neighbourhood, shops, restaurants, and public parks (third place). Interactions with people in these third places can facilitate social relationships and enhance a

60 *Home as relationships*

sense of community. For example, Walker and Hiller (2007) explored the social and physical dimensions of neighbourhoods from the experience of older women in Adelaide, Australia. Their findings show that those women's sense of satisfaction with and confidence in getting out of the house to connect with others is underpinned by trusting and reciprocal relationships with their neighbours. Further support to this conclusion came from a study on the relationship between daily interactions with weak ties (e.g., acquaintances such as neighbours, colleagues, or people encountered in public places like gyms or shops) and psychological well-being (Sandstrom & Dunn, 2014). The findings of this study based on data collected from university students and community members revealed that participants experienced greater happiness and feelings of belonging on days when there were more interactions with weak ties. Therefore, this study highlights the power of weak ties, suggesting that even social interactions with the more peripheral members of our social networks can contribute to well-being.

Family relationships signifying home

Family members and intergenerational relationships play a pivotal role in making people feel at home. When asked about what home means to them, the first thing participants mentioned was family. One recurring theme emerging from the interviews with older Chinese participants is that their home is where their children are. One participant who migrated to Australia in 2004 to join his only daughter described his view of what makes a home this way,

> My family in Australia is 100% my home. Before my daughter came here, we lived in Beijing together as one family. Later she came to Australia to study, we reunited here as a family. The meaning of family for me is blood ties and kinship; they are the most important thing for developing belonging.
>
> (B16, male, aged 81)

The importance of blood ties emerged as a strongly held value among many older Chinese participants. This is further illustrated by words from one participant who explained that his Australian sense of home grew stronger when he moved to Australia to join his daughter, and his Chinese sense of home grew weaker when his connections with relatives in China decreased,

> I used to live with my daughter in China; I felt a sense of home there. Later my daughter moved to Australia; I moved to here, too, to join her.

Home as relationships 61

I feel here is my home now. Several of my old friends and acquaintances passed away. I have very little contact [with old friends back in China]. My brother and sister are not in Hefei [hometown in China]. They are in their late 80s, and can't live independently. I'm here and can't give them much help, and our contact gradually decreased.

(B14, male, aged 83)

Similar to place attachment, the findings showed that blood ties, that is, where their children reside, greatly contribute to a sense of belonging. Moreover, other older Chinese migrants recognise that part of their home is in China because it is their "birthplace" (B12, male, aged 71) or "where all my roots are" (B07, female, aged 60). The fluidity of the notion of home suggests that the construction of home is always in co-existence with the sense of home in the old country and in the new country. It is neither completely here nor completely there. Nevertheless, the sense of belonging to China tends to decrease for those who no longer have relatives in China, especially when their children are all in Australia. A participant who moved to Australia 14 years ago to join her daughter's family told us,

I don't have a home in China any more, no relatives, only a few friends, and some pensions. I have already purchased my own graveyard here. I will spend the rest of my life here. . . . Blood ties are most important.

(B13, female, aged 78)

For the older Chinese who have lived in Australia for several decades, a general sense of belonging to their new home was closely related to having children who grew up in Australia, in addition to factors such as their length of residence, citizenship, and owning a house in Australia. For example, "I have a strong sense of belonging to Australia because of my children, grandchildren, and wife are all here" (A19, male, aged 62); "I call Australia home and I have a very strong sense of belonging because my children all grew up here and work here. They are well integrated here. Australia is my home" (A05, female, aged 60); "After I settled down in Australia and my children went to school, Australia became my home" (A06, male, aged 64). Those quotes again reinforce the view that a strong sense of belonging to Australia is derived primarily from family, similar to a sense of home. For many, the fact that family members are in Australia "planted roots" for place attachment and place identity (A11, female, aged 70). Similarly, another participant (A10, female, aged 66) described her immigration to Australia as, "growing roots" (*luo di sheng gen*), meaning when they stepped on the new land of Australia, they planted roots in the new soil. Hence, they belong to where the roots have grown. These findings suggest that children are

62 Home as relationships

central to the development of feelings of belonging to the new country for migrants because their children provide a bridge between the older country and the new country.

The importance of harmonious relationships among family members, particularly in intergenerational relationships, has been emphasised by several older Chinese migrants we interviewed. As the Chinese saying goes, "everything prospers in a harmonious family". At the time of the study, many older Chinese participants lived with their adult children, oftentimes, with grandchildren as well. The sense of home embodied many Chinese cultural elements that older generations wish to pass on to younger

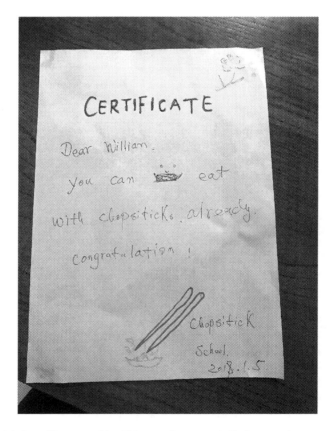

Photo 4.1 A certificate an older Chinese migrant made for her grandson to congratulate him on having mastered the skill of using chopsticks to eat meals, a Chinese tradition.

Source: Shuang Liu. Used with permission.

Home as relationships 63

generations. Examples are observation of traditional values (e.g., respect for seniority) and beliefs (e.g., relying on herbal medicine to maintain health and treat illness), celebration of traditional festivals (e.g., Chinese lunar new year), pay tribute to ancestors, eating Chinese food, and using the Chinese language for communication. It is emotionally comforting for older Chinese migrants to live with family members who share a cultural heritage and practice passed on from generation to generation. As such they want their younger generations to be able to speak the Chinese language and to carry on Chinese cultural traditions, no matter how "Australian" they have become because they *are* Chinese.

While children, grandchildren, and harmonious intergenerational relationships play a pivotal role in cultivating a sense of home for older family members, they are clearly aware of the cultural change in younger generations, for example, the changed understanding of filial piety. Traditionally, Confucian cultural values of family care encouraged older Chinese people's dependence on their children and reduced their desire to seek assistance from formal care providers (Park & Kim, 2013). Many older Chinese felt that since they sacrificed their personal interest for the betterment of their children (e.g., working to provide better education for their children) when they were young, a reciprocal filial obligation was due from their adult children to care for them in their later life. However, such expectations were often not shared by younger generations who viewed their roles of caring for their older parents more in the provision of financial support, rather than fulfilling the role of a personal carer (Mui & Kang, 2006). Recognising that social norms associated with the tradition of filial piety have changed, the older Chinese participants accept and some even embrace the concept that they "need to be more independent" (A01, male, aged 59); "when I become too old to look after myself, I would move to an aged care facility" (A11, female, aged 70). These discussions with younger generations may take place at home and in a positive communication climate whereas, in the past, such conversations were more likely to have been avoided as going to an aged-care facility was traditionally interpreted as familial rejection (Chow, 2004). One participant, who migrated to Australia in 2013 to join her daughter and lived with her daughter in the same apartment at the time of the interview, told us that she did not mind going to an aged-care facility, but she hopes that they have Chinese services [meaning Chinese speakers] (B02, female, aged 78). Another participant who has lived in Australia since 1975 expressed that he is open-minded to the view of going to an aged-care facility, but also indicated that it is not a common practice among his friends,

I have lived here for over 40 years. I feel very safe here. People here are very friendly. Brisbane has the best climate. I can drive, have my own

64 *Home as relationships*

car, and feel life here is very convenient. I can do anything I want to. I can accept going to an aged-care facility or a retirement home, but no one around me lives in an aged-care facility.

(B04, male, aged 78)

Many participants are grateful for the good healthcare system and high-quality living conditions in retirement villages in Australia. However, they expressed concerns over a lack of Chinese-speaking staff and services in Australian aged-care facilities. On the one hand, they accept the idea of going into aged care facilities but, on the other hand, they try to push the prospect as far into the future as possible, believing that the best place to spend their late years is at home, preferably with children and grandchildren nearby.

Social relationships signifying home

Social networks always play an important role in the life of Chinese people. Generational differences at home, in a way, made older Chinese migrants in Australia more aware of the importance of building new social networks with their co-ethnics in the host country because the opportunity to share cultural practices and even personal experiences is emotionally comforting. Most participants regularly participate in community activities that predominantly only involve people from their own Chinese ethnic groups. They feel that connections with the Chinese communities, friends, and the neighbourhood helped and continue to help them to build a sense of home in Australia. Most of them kept regular contacts with friends through activities such as weekly gatherings at church, dining out together or yum cha (having tea in a Chinese restaurant) weekly or fortnightly, or visiting each other's home if they live within walking distance. Their social networks seemed to be entirely made up of friends with the same Chinese ethnic background. The purpose of gathering together, as they expressed, was to interact with friends to learn about what was going on. A participant who moved to Australia in 2013 to look after her daughter showed us a photograph taken with a group of friends dining in a Chinese restaurant, and described the importance of friends to her this way,

I often go for outings with friends; I participate in some activities organised by Chinese here almost daily. I've made some new friends who live nearby. This shows that I am not just a lonely individual. Although I have only one daughter, I have many friends to keep me company.

(B02, female, aged 78)

Home as relationships 65

Similarly, another participant showed us a photograph of Chinese from her hometown in China gathering together at a social event, and explained,

> This photograph was taken at the gathering of people who came from my hometown in China. We are from Hunan Province in China. Our Hunan Hometown Association (Hunan Tong Xiang Hui) has more than 400 members. We often meet together for social activities, organised by our association. This photograph was our "Red Chilli Gathering" [Hunan Province in China is known for its large consumption of chilli and spicy food]. You see, we were all wearing the uniforms of our hometown association.
>
> (B11, female, aged 65)

The participant further added that people from their association regularly gather in a Chinese restaurant, which specialises in authentic Hunan cuisine. Since they all came from the same hometown and of similar age, this similarity in culture and background gives them a lot to talk to each other. For some special cultural festivals such as the mid-autumn festival or the Chinese New Year, they usually have a bigger gathering in that restaurant to celebrate. These quotes indicate that friendships provide an emotional support network for ageing migrants, as well as a source of identity and belonging. As Wiles and colleagues (2012) found in their study, friendships and connections within migrants' associations function as an important resource, or even safety net, for older people, who live in their homes and communities. In addition, the opportunity to talk with co-ethnics of the same age offers a unique kind of social connectedness which talking with family members may not be able to offer.

Churches or temples also provide a social and cultural place for older Chinese to gather with friends and opportunities for older Chinese migrants to give and receive emotional support. One participant described her experience this way,

> I regularly gather with my friends; we participate in church activities together, and we visit each other's homes about once a week or once per fortnight. Face-to-face meetings express sincerity; we use our own action to show care and love to each other.
>
> (A02, female, aged 61)

On the other hand, a lack of social support from friends and social networks can result in loneliness and low psychological well-being. As one participant expressed,

66 Home as relationships

Photo 4.2 Chung Tian Temple, "Middle Heaven", in Brisbane is a place of worship for many Chinese migrants, particularly Buddhists.
Source: Siqin Wang. Used with permission.

> My husband passed away. My two sons are both here; thus, I can only stay here. This townhouse, located in the centre of Toowoomba city [a regional city in Queensland], is supplied by the Government. I live here by myself. . . . I'm the only Chinese in the local community; others are all foreigners [non-Chinese] . . . I don't speak English, can't talk to others. I feel very lonely.
>
> (B17, female, aged 82)

This quote pointed out the link between connectedness with people and connectedness with the physical environment. The fact is that living alone at home, which is located in a neighbourhood with hardly any Chinese co-ethnics, and a lack of English language proficiency restricted her physical mobility. The limited ability to navigate the neighbourhood further constrains her social mobility, such as making friends, or meeting with friends, or participating in social activities. This combination of factors contributes to her feeling of loneliness and social isolation. In contrast, other older

Home as relationships 67

Chinese we interviewed, who are more socially connected, tend to live in or near Chinese-concentrated suburbs, with Chinese restaurants, grocery stores, doctor's place, and their friends' houses nearby. Several participants who used to live in suburbs lightly populated by Chinese migrants later moved to Chinese-concentrated suburbs, such as Sunnybank and Sunnybank Hills in Brisbane, because they can walk to Chinese restaurants for gathering with friends without having to bother their children to provide transportation. One participant who moved to Australia in 2004 to join her daughter's family explained,

We all live here [Sunnybank – a Chinese concentrated suburb] and we can walk to each other's home [friends]. It only takes a couple of minutes to walk to the Chinese stores and restaurants from where we live. Previously we stayed with our children in Holland Park [a suburb in Brisbane] and it was very inconvenient because we had to rely on our children to drive us around if we wanted to go anywhere. Since we moved back to Sunnybank, we don't want to move to other suburbs anymore because we are close to restaurants, stores, supermarkets, and close to our friends, too.

(B13, female, aged 78)

One regular social activity that the older Chinese migrants in our study enjoy doing is meeting with family and friends in a Chinese restaurant. Chinese restaurants are places where Chinese extended families enjoy family time during weekends. Most of the older Chinese from Mainland China came to Australia for the primary purpose of helping to take care of their grandchildren who were born and raised in Australia. As the second-generation Chinese migrants, their grandchildren are growing up in the bicultural context. Family gathering in a Chinese restaurant serves as not only a means of enjoying Chinese food, but also a medium to pass on the Chinese food culture to the next generation. Moreover, a Chinese restaurant is a social and cultural space where older Chinese meet old friends, make new friends, learn about what is going on in Australia and their local areas, and give and receive social support from network of friends. For example, a participant from Hong Kong, who had lived in Australia for more than three decades told us,

As a Hong Konger, we came to Yam Chai [a typical Cantonese restaurant) three or four times a week, and spend half day on drinking tea, eating dim sum [Cantonese style appetizers) and chatting with friends. The restaurant boss knows us very well and always gives us discount.

68 *Home as relationships*

Here [Yam Chai] is the social place for us to connect with friends especially from Hong Kong, Guangzhou, or Malaysia.

(04, male, aged 78)

Restaurants also serve as a platform for connecting their old country with the new country because it is usually the place where older Chinese entertain visitors from their old country, as described by this participant,

This is a photograph taken in a Chinese restaurant when my friends from China last visited us in Brisbane. When my old friends from China come to visit me, I always take them to a local Chinese restaurant so that we can chat over a nice meal.

(B15, female, aged 78)

Friendship may play a more important role in emotional and social support, particularly for those older Chinese who experience conflicts in intergenerational relationships at home. The opportunity to talk through even some unhappy experiences could help to reduce pressure because of the emotional support from peers. Hence, Chinese restaurants have become a cultural place for them to meet and connect with friends, treating friends from the old home country to a good meal, giving and receiving social support, and expanding social networks by making new friends.

The research findings identified relationships with people in the neighbourhood or even people working at services in shops or restaurants as contributing to migrants' sense of home in Australia. These kind of relationships are not based upon kinship, nor social networks, but nevertheless play a role in making them feel at home. When asked about what they like about life in Australia as an older person, several participants mentioned the relaxed lifestyle in Australia in contrast to the fast-paced life in China, clean air, good health system, and quality of living conditions. In addition to lifestyle change, which gives them satisfaction in life (Benson & O'Reilly, 2009), what they find most happy with is the friendly Australian people they encounter in the neighbourhood, at various service places, such as doctors, shop assistants at checkout counters, or even bus drivers. Some participants commented that "my neighbours are very friendly", "we neighbours help each other", and "everyone is equal here". Even a simple greeting like "hello" said in Chinese by a local Australian would give them a sense of home and a feeling of belonging to the community. One participant who had lived in Australia for 34 years described her feeling of home,

I'm very satisfied with my life in Australia. I have a comfortable house to live in. House symbolises home, and home is in the house. I have a

Home as relationships 69

sense of home in my neighbourhood. In general, Australians are very accommodating to foreigners. I enjoy the feeling of being accepted here. It is also very important that family members respect each other and live in harmony. Family members should care for each other, accepting each other. Only when there is love in the family, it is home.

(A02, female, aged 61)

This quote points to several dimensions of home: ownership of a property, location, friendly neighbourhood, accommodating attitudes to foreigners by the larger society, as well as love, respect, and acceptance among family members. All of those elements collectively contribute to a sense of home in Australia.

Conclusion

This chapter explores the concept of home as a set of relationships. As a social and cultural space, home entails a set of relationships, such as relationships with family including intergenerational relationships, relationships with friends in social networks, and relationship with others in the neighbourhood. The empirical data from interviews with older Chinese participants and the photographs show that it is through family and social relationships that older Chinese migrants develop social and cultural insidedness, integrating into the social and cultural environment through everyday interactions with people and the environment. Moreover, this chapter echoes the argument that it is not only interactions with strong ties (e.g., family and friends) that have the most influence in one's sense of connectedness with their environment. Equally as significant are those interactions with more peripheral members of the social networks (e.g., neighbours and acquaintances) that are typically characterised by weak ties, but which still can have the power to enhance a sense of community and well-being (Sandstrom & Dunn, 2014). Therefore, it is through family, social, and cultural relationships that older Chinese migrants develop a sense of home, identity, and belonging in Australia.

A Chinese migrant's home is a place where traditional culture is maintained, practised, and passed on to younger generations. However, along with cultural maintenance, home was also seen as a place in which cultural shifting is manifested in younger generations, including the grandchildren who were born in Australia. Hence, both home and host cultures were always at play in the family context. Generational differences in adherence to traditional cultural values and practices are felt among older Chinese migrants, especially among those older Chinese who live with their adult children and grandchildren in the same household. For example, the concept of filial

70 *Home as relationships*

piety has changed among adult children who have acculturated at a faster speed than the older generation and are more oriented towards individualistic culture of the host country (Lin et al., 2016). Older Chinese migrants realise the need to adjust to change in the practice of filial piety, as they acculturate into the host country themselves, albeit at a slower speed than their younger generations.

The awareness of generational differences at home encouraged older Chinese to see the importance of building new social networks with their co-ethnics in the host country. They feel friendships with co-ethnics of similar age and background can be an important source of emotional and social support. Many of the participants made new friends since they migrated to Australia, through going to churches, temples, and participating in social activities organised by Chinese community associations. The opportunities to share old life experiences in the old country, to celebrate cultural festivals, birthdays, and even to talk about not-so-happy experiences at home, such as intergenerational conflicts, can be emotionally rewarding. Most participants regularly participate in community activities, predominantly only involving people from their own Chinese ethnic groups, such as going to a Chinese Buddhist temple. At the same time, they maintained contacts with old friends in the home country and welcomed the opportunities to catch up with old friends when they visited them in Australia. These findings highlight the importance of social and cultural insideness in enacting a sense of home.

Social networks, the matrix of social relationships within which individuals operate, have been found to constitute an essential component of successful ageing by providing individuals with social embeddedness and engagement (Cornwell, Laumann, & Schumm, 2008). The role of strong social ties has been suggested as especially critical for older immigrant populations because they experience disruptions in traditional social networks in the process of immigration and settling into the society that is linguistically and culturally different from their native countries (Dong, Chang, Wong, & Simon, 2012). Participants emphasised the importance of self-reliance and the ability to seek social support from sources outside the family. To this end, they expanded their social network but only to include ethnic community organisations and churches that had services available in Chinese language. The social support gained from a large network can provide individuals meaning and purpose in life, promoting a sense of home, and allows integration into the larger society, thus influencing health and well-being (Su & Ferraro, 1997). Moreover, social connections are extended to neighbours. Previous research has shown that a greater number of daily interactions with others, even those who were not close network members, was associated with higher levels well-being (Sandstrom &

Home as relationships 71

Dunn, 2014). In a family-centred culture like the Chinese culture, the quality of intergenerational relationships, the size of social networks, and the level of engagement in social activities collectively play a significant role in reducing social isolation and increasing social connectedness among older Chinese migrants, thereby building their social and cultural insideness in the host country. The next chapter extends this idea and explores home as a transnational place.

References

Benson, M., & O'Reilly, K. (2009). Migration and the search for a better way of life: A critical exploration of lifestyle migration. *Sociological Review*, *57*(4), 608–625.

Chow, N. (2004). Asian value and aged care. *Geriatrics and Gerontology International*, *4*(1), 21–25.

Cornwell, B., Laumann, E. O., & Schumm, L. P. (2008). The social connectedness of older adults: A national profile. *American Sociological Review*, *73*(2), 185–203.

Department of Home Affairs. (2019). Explore visa options for joining family in Australia. Retrieved from https://immi.homeaffairs.gov.au/visas/getting-a-visa/visa-finder/join-family.

Dong, X., Wong, E., & Simon, M. (2012). A qualitative study of filial piety among community dwelling, Chinese, older adults: Changing meaning and impact on health and well-being. *Journal of Intergenerational Relationships*, *10*, 131–146.

Gardner, P. J. (2011). Natural neighbourhood networks: Important social networks in the lives of older adults aging in place. *Journal of Aging Studies*, *25*, 263–271.

Hodge, A. M., English, D. R., Giles, G. G., & Flicker, L. (2013). Social connectedness and predictors of successful ageing. *Maturitas*, *75*(4), 361–366.

Hwang, K-K. (1999). Filial piety and loyalty: Two types of social identification in Confucianism. *Asian Journal of Social Psychology*, *2*, 163–183.

Ip, D., Lui, C. W., & Chui, W. H. (2007). Veiled entrapment: A study of social isolation of older Chinese migrants in Brisbane, Queensland. *Ageing & Society*, *27*, 719–738.

Ketrow, S. M., & DiCioccio, R. L. (2009). Family interaction in consequential or crisis decisions. *China Media Research*, *5*(1), 81–86.

Li, W. W., & Chong, M. D. (2012). Transnationalism, social wellbeing and older Chinese migrants. *Graduate Journal of Asia-Pacific Studies*, *8*(1), 29–44.

Lin, X., Bryant, C., Boldero, J., & Dow, B. (2015). Older Chinese immigrants' relationships with their children: A literature review from a solidarity-conflict perspective. *The Gerontologist*, *55*(6), 990–1005.

Lin, X., Bryant, C., Boldero, J., & Dow, B. (2016). Psychological well-being of older Chinese immigrants living in Australia: A comparison with older Caucasians. *International Psychogeriatrics*, *28*(10), 1671–1679.

Meijering, L., & Lager, D. (2014). Home-making of older Antillean migrants in the Netherlands. *Ageing & Society*, *34*, 859–875.

Mui, A. C., & Kang, S-Y. (2006). Acculturation stress and depression among Asian immigrant elders. *Social Work*, *51*(3), 243–255.

72 Home as relationships

Park, H-J., & Kim, C. (2013). Ageing in an inconvenient paradise: The immigrant experiences of older Korean people in New Zealand. *Australasian Journal on Ageing, 32,* 158–162.

Park, H-J., Morgan, T., Wiles, J., & Gott, M. (2019). Lonely ageing in a foreign land: Social isolation and loneliness among older Asian migrants in New Zealand. *Health and Social Care Community, 27*(3), 740–747. https://doi.org/10/1111/hsc.12690

Register, M. E., & Herman, J. (2010). Quality of life revisited: The concept of connectedness in older adults. *Advances in Nursing Science, 33,* 53–63.

Sandstrom, G. M., & Dunn, E. W. (2014). Social interactions and well-being: The surprising power of weak ties. *Personality and Social Psychology Bulletin, 40,* 910–922.

Shankar, A., Rafnsson, S. B., & Steptoe, A. (2015). Longitudinal associations between social connections and subjective wellbeing in the English Longitudinal Study of Ageing. *Psychology & Health, 30*(6), 686–698.

Su, Y., & Ferraro, K. (1997). Social relations and health assessments among older people: Do the effects of integration and social contributions vary cross-culturally? *Journal of Gerontology: Social Sciences, 52B,* S27-S36.

Treas, J., & Mazumdar, S. (2002). Older people in America's immigrant families: Dilemmas of dependence, integration, and isolation. *Journal of Aging Studies, 16,* 243–258.

Wahl, N-W., & Oswald, F. (2010). Environmental perspectives on ageing. In D. Dannefer & C. Phillipson (Eds.), *The Sage handbook of social gerontology* (pp. 111–124). London: Sage.

Walker, R. B., & Hiller, J. E. (2007). Places and health: A qualitative study to explore how older women living alone perceive the social and physical dimensions of their neighbourhoods. *Social Science & Medicine, 65*(6), 1154–1165.

Ward, C., & Lin, E-Y. (2010). There are homes at the four corners of the seas: Acculturation and adaptation of overseas Chinese. In M. H. Bond (Ed.), *The Oxford handbook of Chinese psychology* (pp. 657–677). Hong Kong: Oxford University Press.

Wiles, J. L., Leibing, A., Guberman, N., Reeve, J., & Allen, R. E. S. (2012). The meaning of "aging in place" to older people. *The Gerontologist, 52*(3), 357–366.

Wong, S. T., Yoo, G. J., & Stewart, A. L. (2006). The changing meaning of family support among older Chinese and Korean immigrants. *Journal of Gerontology, 61B*(1), S4-S9.

Yuval-Davis, N. (2010). Theorizing identity: Beyond the "us" and "them" dichotomy. *Patterns of Prejudice, 44*(3), 261–280.

Zhan, H., Wang, Q., Fawcett, Z., Li, X., & Fan, X. (2017). Finding a sense of home across the Pacific in old age: Chinese American senior's report of life satisfaction in a foreign land. *Journal of Cross Cultural Gerontology, 32,* 31–55.

5 Home as a transnational place
Autobiographical insideness

Introduction

Migrants across the world form diaspora communities in their settlement country. The term *diaspora* is based on the Greek terms *speiro*, meaning "to sow" and the preposition *dia*, meaning "over". The Greeks used diaspora to refer to migration and colonisation. In Hebrew, the term initially referred to the settling of scattered colonies of Jews outside Palestine after the Babylonian exile, and came to have a more general connotation of people settled away from their ancestral homeland. The meaning of diaspora has shifted over time and now refers not only to traditional migrant groups, such as Jews, but also much wider communities comprised of voluntary migrants living in more than one culture (Clifford, 1997). Many migrants today build their diaspora community in the host country, with social networks crossing home country and host country. The process by which migrants forge and sustain multi-stranded social relations that link together their societies of origin and settlement is referred to as transnationalism (Baldassar, Pyke, & Ben-Moshe, 2017). In this sense, the practice of transnationalism functions as a vehicle for the transmission and maintenance of heritage culture and language in the host country (Siu, 2005). Today, diaspora and transnational ties are more easily maintained, thanks to advancement in communication technologies, smartphones, internet-enabled devices, and digital media. As migrants maintain transnational contacts, they continuously negotiate identities between "old" and "new" countries, creating new configurations of identification with home in both places. It is through this maintenance of border-spanning multiple relationships – familial, economic, social, cultural, religious, and political – that migrants or transmigrants develop their identity, belonging, and emotional bond with both home country and host country.

This chapter concentrates on home as a transnational place for older Chinese migrants and explores how they develop autobiographic insideness – the

74 *Home as a transnational place*

sense of identity, belonging, and emotional bond with a place that is developed through older people's cumulative experiences of living in a particular place (Rowles, 1983). The chapter first reviews theories and previous research on transnationalism and transnational community. Drawing on empirical data from interviews with older Chinese participants and engaging with the photographs they supplied, the chapter next illustrates how older Chinese migrants negotiate identity and belonging in the process of building a sense of home as their life is straddled between China and Australia. The participants described their identity as Chinese-Australian. This dual cultural affiliation is reflected in their intergenerational relationships, interaction with old friends in China and new friends in Australia, as well as their engagement in social activities organised by Chinese migrant communities. Moreover, participants have indicated change in their identity and belonging since they moved to Australia. Such change is particularly felt when they interact with old friends in China or when they return to China for a visit. This chapter highlights the dynamic nature of identity and belonging among older Chinese migrants and the complexities of the concept of autobiographical insideness in migrants who live in a transnational place of their own creation.

Chinese diaspora and transnational community

The term "Chinese diaspora" has been commonly used to refer broadly to Chinese overseas. In the Euro-American countries the term has been used to refer to those Chinese living outside mainland China, Hong Kong, Macau, and Taiwan, all of which can be described as the Chinese lands (Tan, 2013). Although the term is commonly applied, in practice what constitutes a diaspora is debatable. Some scholars argue that descendants who have become rooted in a country and integrated into that society should no longer be considered as diaspora members (Cohen, 2008); others contend that local-born second, third, and fourth generation migrants should still be considered as members of the diasporic community due to their cultural ancestry (Ang, 2014). Globalisation, too, blurs the boundaries of diaspora and non-diaspora space. Take the example of a multicultural city like Sydney. As a global city in Australia, it receives the largest proportion of migrants of Chinese descent from mainland China, Taiwan, Hong Kong, Malaysia, Singapore, Vietnam, and East Timor, as well as those younger migrant generations who were born in Australia. All of them consider themselves "Chinese" and come to share the social and cultural space where Chinese in Australia intersect and interact. As a result, scholars researching on diasporas are increasingly interested in diaspora discourses instead of being concerned about what precisely constitutes a diaspora, paying more attention

Home as a transnational place 75

to experiences "of constructing homes away from home" (Clifford, 1997, p. 244). Nevertheless, this chapter operationally defines Chinese diaspora as Chinese from mainland China, Hong Kong, Macau, and Taiwan, since this definition aligns with the background of the older Chinese participants from whom we collected empirical data.

Regardless of their reasons for migrating, migrants of all ethnic backgrounds form their diaspora communities in the host country because such communities provide a useful platform to link the country of origin to the country in which they presently reside. In this sense, diasporic communities are transnational communities, which serve to facilitate processes of resettlement, cross-cultural adjustment, and integration in the host country (Li & Chong, 2012). Homeland connections play a crucial role in reminding migrants of their transnational relationship with their place of origin, which is not simply somewhere they have left behind, but rather a place of continuing attachment after they have geographically located elsewhere (Clifford, 1994). Migrants or transmigrants who move, physically or virtually, between old and new cultures and countries maintain homes in both places and pursue social, economic, political, and cultural interests that require their presence in both countries or cultures (Portes, 1997). Transnationalism therefore describes the process through which migrants and transmigrants build, maintain, and reinforce multiple economic, social, cultural, and emotional interconnections with more than one place (Green, Power, & Jang, 2008).

Traditionally, the predominant belief among social scientists appears to be that identity boundaries are something everyone both experiences, and ought to feel reluctant to change or compromise (Kim, 1994). Identity and group membership are explained in terms of dualities, that is, we define what and who we are vis-à-vis what and who we are not (Tajfel & Turner, 1979). In an era of increasing intercultural contact and cross-border mobility, the complexities of cultural identity defy the neat boundaries of this dichotomous conception because it overlooks the fact that people have multiple cultural identities (Liu, 2015a). For example, the immigration journey of the early waves of Chinese migrants to Australia in the 1800s involved a movement away from home culture and assimilation to the White Australian society to the furthest extent possible. Contemporary Chinese migrants travel back and forth and between their country of origin and country of settlement, inhibit multiple homes, perform different roles, and speak more than one language. Instead of being pressured to assimilate into the mainstream culture, they construct bicultural or multicultural identities, create social networks in both cultures, and transform their cultural practices in both home and host countries. Cultural theorist Stuart Hall (1990), who has written extensively about transnational migration and diasporic cultures, challenges the essentialist, fixed, ahistorical conceptions of identity

76 *Home as a transnational place*

by arguing that cultural identity is not an essence but a positioning. Such argument sheds light on our understanding of transnationalism and migrant identities.

Erving Goffman (1969) defines identity as the way in which individuals manage their self-image and perform to the expectations of others in everyday life. The fluid nature of identity has long been recognised in the literature, dating back to the twentieth century when distinguished American sociologist and psychologist Margaret Mead (1934), among other earlier researchers in the field, described it as a dynamic process. According to this perspective, identity is not something "given" but is constructed in acts of social interaction. Immigrants' identity is shaped by the specific political and economic circumstances under which particular beliefs and practices serve as boundary markers. When boundaries expand and markers change, immigrants need to reconstruct their identities and re-negotiate their place in the larger society. For example, the policy of Anglo-conformity in post–World War II Australia demanded immigrants' complete renunciation of their heritage culture in favour of the behaviour and values of the Anglo-Saxon group. Non-White migrants such as Asians were expected to meet expectations imposed upon them to become "new Australians" (Brockhall & Liu, 2011). Since the abolishment of the White Australia policy and the implementation of multiculturalism in Australia in the 1970s, migrants are encouraged to retain their own ethnic cultural practices while participating in the mainstream society. As they live and move in-between cultures, they (re)construct bicultural identities, albeit different forms of bicultural identities. In this respect, identity negotiation for migrants is a continuous process of adaptation and negotiation, leading to cultural acceptance and coherence (Huang, 2011).

Identity negotiation takes place in the context of communicating with others and there are many elements of identity that are intrinsically linked with social expectations and contexts (Hecht, Warren, Jung, & Krieger, 2005). Social actors use linguistic and other cultural resources in the ongoing construction and reconstruction of personal and collective identity. In her identity negotiation theory, Ting-Toomey (2005) states that identity is viewed as reflective self-images constructed, experienced, and communicated by the individuals in a particular interaction situation within a cultural context. The concept of negotiation is defined as "a transactional interaction process whereby individuals in an intercultural situation attempt to assert, define, modify, challenge and/or support their own and others' desired self-images" (Ting-Toomey, 2005, p. 217). While an individual is free to create multiple selves, there are various personal and social constraints with regard to the possible selves one can negotiate: "what they might become, what they would like to become, and what they are afraid of becoming" (Markus &

Home as a transnational place 77

Nurius, 1986, p. 954). The categories an individual uses to define his or her identity and belonging symbolically marks the boundaries between the self and the other. Previous research suggests that hyphenated identity, for example, Chinese-Australian, is most preferred by migrants, particularly long-term migrants (Liu, 2015b). However, dual cultural identification is not necessarily characterised by an equal level of attachment to or identification with both cultures. This view has been supported by previous research on Chinese-Canadians and Chinese-Dutch. In studying hyphenated identities among the second-generation Chinese in Canada and the Netherlands, Bélanger and Verkuyten (2010) argued that hyphenated identities should not simply be equated with integrated acculturation profile, which means identification with both home and host cultures. The findings show that individuals may perform to the expectations of the culture and lifestyle of the majority group in the host country, and yet identify strongly with their ethnic culture. Similarly, findings from another study on Vietnamese migrants revealed a clear difference between identifying as Vietnamese and feelings of closeness to Vietnam (Baldassar et al., 2017). Based on a survey to 466 participants of Vietnamese background in Australia, followed by two focus groups, with six participants in each, the researchers conclude that the participants' sense of Vietnamese identity is relatively strong, whereas their feelings of closeness to Vietnam is relatively weak. Although this study did not specifically target older migrants, the findings shed light on a possible distinction between identification with a culture and strength of ties to that culture.

Transnational connections with the homeland are made significantly easier thanks to the advancements in communication technologies. The evolution of digital media supports the processes of transnationalism and allows migrants to engage in immediate, frequent, and continuous contact with their homeland. Smartphones, for example, have become a necessity for communication within and across geographical borders, although the frequency of contact with family and friends may depend on the size of an individual's social network and whether or not they have family members still living in the home country. In addition to interpersonal contact, as Siu (2005) found in the case of Chinese diaspora in South America, the rapid increase in the distribution of transnational Chinese media products, such as news, movies, and TV soap operas, expands the resources available for Chinese diasporic identification by providing greater opportunities to link life in the two countries. The study conducted on Vietnamese migrants in Australia further echoes the idea that diaspora identity can be sustained and renewed by transnational communication technologies and media produced in Hong Kong, Canada, and America (Baldassar et al., 2017). As such, electronic networks

78 *Home as a transnational place*

such as the internet relate migrants socially and emotionally to both their home and host countries (Lim, Bork-Hüffer, & Yeoh, 2016). These transnational connections provide a useful lens for understanding the development of autobiographical insideness in the context of transnational communities. While autobiographical insidedness is derived from a sense of identity that an older person has developed through the cumulative experiences of living in a place (Wahl & Oswald, 2010), the creation of transnational identity provides a continuity between the old self and the present self, bridging past life in the home country and the present life in the host country.

Transnational identity and belonging signifying home

In terms of cultural identification, the empirical findings from interviews with older Chinese participants show that majority self-identified as Chinese-Australian, a few as Chinese, while none self-identified as Australian only. These older Chinese migrants recognise elements of heritage and host cultures in their hyphenated identity of Chinese-Australian. However, the Chinese and the Australian components of their cultural identity are derived from different sources. One participant who migrated to Australia in 2004 when he was 67 years old described his cultural identification this way,

> I identify culturally as a Chinese-Australian because I migrated to Australia and have lived in this country for so long. However, my appearance is Chinese. This represents me as one of the Chinese people. Australia is a country I live in.
>
> (B16, male, aged 81)

Similarly, another older participant who also made the immigration journey later in life at the age of 46, and has lived in Australia for close to 30 years expressed,

> I see myself as a Chinese-Australian. I was brought up as Chinese. After I lived in Australia for so long, I became Australianised. Yes, I'm an Australian. I hold an Australian passport and own a house in Australia, but I'm also Chinese.
>
> (A04, male, aged 73)

These quotes show that the Australian components of their identity tend to be related to being an Australian citizen, or long-term residence in Australia. Other participants explained that they identify as Chinese-Australian because their children were born and grew up in the country, or they own a house in Australia. In contrast, when we asked them about what made them *feel*

Home as a transnational place 79

Chinese in Australia, instead of citizenship and place of permanent residence, reasons associated with cultural heritage, food, tradition, language, physical appearances, and cultural roots were instead predominant. These components of identity seem to be related to something much deeper, and something that cannot be changed. Moreover, participants consider their hyphenated identity as involving the coexistence, rather than the merging, of home and host cultures. Nevertheless, similar to previous research on Vietnamese migrants in Australia (Baldassar et al., 2017), participants in our study did not perceive incompatibility of the two cultures in their cultural identification.

In relation to the reasons for belonging, participants tend to relate their belonging to Australia with long periods of residence in the host country and holding an Australian passport (A07, male, aged 86), factors similarly mentioned in reference to their cultural identification. Participants expressed pride in being an Australian citizen, which afforded them a quality living standard, fresh air, friendly people, good health care facilities, social security (A08, female, aged 78), and established legal systems (A12, female, aged 63). However, while Chinese-Australian emerges as the most preferred cultural identity, the strength of belonging to Australia varies among older Chinese. In particular, when going beyond the family context to situate belonging in the larger social context, the feelings of belonging become mixed. One participant who migrated to Australia at the age of 28, and has lived in Australia for 38 years, explained why she does not have a strong sense of belonging to Australia,

> I don't have a strong sense of belonging to Australia. You say Australia is my country; it is not really 100% because my language is primarily Chinese. You say I don't have a sense of belonging to Australia, it is not true. I enjoy living in Australia. I've lived here for over 30 years, longer than I had lived in Hong Kong. I'm an Australian citizen.
>
> (A16, female, aged 66)

This participant's words reveal that her sense of belonging seems to be more closely related to language, a medium through which the heritage Chinese culture is maintained. She also made an interesting distinction between identity and belonging. While belonging is a more subjective sense or feeling, identity is not always self-defined as it can be ascribed by others. Another participant who had lived in Australia for 16 years described her experience this way,

> I have a sense of belonging to Australia, but not very strong. Of course, it depends on the context. Identity sometimes is not decided by yourself. You think you are an Australian, but others may not think so.

80 *Home as a transnational place*

Citizenship is an important factor for identifying as an Australian, but appearance and way of life make me feel I'm not an Australian.

(A20, female, aged 56)

Clearly, ethnic language (Mandarin or Cantonese) and ethnic physical appearance are considered by those Chinese participants as markers of Chineseness. However, cultural traits that bind migrants together may also be used to set them apart from mainstream Australian society. A consequence can be feelings of social isolation among some older Chinese, as one participant who migrated to Australia 26 years ago vividly described her feeling this way,

The weather, heath care facilities, and social welfare systems are all very good in Australia. It is a good place for older people to spend their late life here. However, because I'm living in a foreign land and don't have many family members, I feel lonely and socially isolated. Just like a tree being replanted into soil of a new environment. It may not necessarily grow better just because the soil is more fertile and the environment is better.

(A07, male, aged 86)

This participant acknowledged the higher level of quality of life in Australia, which he really appreciates and values. On the other hand, he expressed the challenges of living in a foreign land, particularly in terms of social isolation due to loss of connections to culture and valued social networks in the home country. The quote shows that continuation of old culture in the new location becomes very important to older Chinese migrants to give them a sense of home in a foreign land. In their eyes, Chinese cultural identity is reflected in adherence to traditional values (e.g., respect for seniority) and beliefs (e.g., eating a balanced diet of "hot" and "cold" food to maintain balance in body systems), family members helping each other (e.g., grandparents helping in the care of grandchildren), and the celebration of traditional festivals (e.g., Chinese new year). As language is integral to culture and identity, older generations of Chinese migrants want their grandchildren, often born in Australia, to see themselves as Chinese and be able to speak the Chinese language. One participant who has continued to teach Chinese since she moved to Australia 14 years ago told us,

I began to teach Chinese since I was 18 years old. I continued to teach Chinese after I moved to Australia. In 2010, I set up my own Chinese school on the ground floor of my house. I live upstairs. I have devoted my entire life to this job. I taught Chinese in China and I teach Chinese

Home as a transnational place 81

in Australia. I hope the Chinese children outside China can speak Chinese and see themselves as Chinese.

(B15, female, aged 78)

Ethnic enclaves help to keep the use of ethnic language alive, and consequently, many Chinese language schools have been established in residential areas densely populated by Chinese migrants in the hope of using the ethnic language to reconnect their younger generations to their "homeland". In addition, many older Chinese migrants consider eating Chinese cuisine at home as another important avenue for preserving their cultural identity. One participant whose son-in-law is Italian showed us a photograph of a family outing and said,

What remains the same in Australia is our food culture. We eat Chinese rice, gluten rice balls and Chinese dumplings when we live in my daughter's house. This gives me a feeling of being a Chinese in Australia. My son-in-law is Italian, but he likes to eat Chinese dumplings.

(B03, female, aged 59)

However, identity incongruence can occur when older Chinese migrants return home for a visit. They treasure old connections, but at the same time, they felt the "distance" between old friends and themselves when returning to their old country. A participant who had lived in Australia for 16 years told us,

Returning home, language is not a problem. However, when I go out to shop or interact with people in China, I feel that there is a screen between them and me. The Chinese in China have different beliefs and norms governing behaviour. Sometimes I feel Australia is better when I am in China.

(A20, female, aged 56)

The sense of being a "visitor" in their home country is accentuated by ascribed cultural identities incongruent with the cultural context. As the same participant related, "I'm seen by Australians as Chinese; when I return to China, my friends see me as Australian". Living in-between cultures can result in difficulties in fitting in either or both cultures. Incongruence between culture and context occurs from time to time as discrepancies between self-defined identity and ascribed identity in either or both cultures arise.

Moreover, the sense of being a "visitor" in their homeland can become stronger for migrants when they do not have a house of their own in the

82 *Home as a transnational place*

home country, as illustrated by a participant who has lived in Australia for 27 years,

> When I go back to my home country for a visit, I feel like a visitor because I no longer have a house in my home country. I have to stay with my relatives, so I'm a guest. My house is in Australia.
>
> (A04, male, aged 73)

In a similar vein, another participant who migrated to Australia from Hong Kong 36 years ago said,

> Indeed, having left China for over 30 years, what I have is only memory [referring to Hong Kong]. There is not much feeling of belonging to Hong Kong. I've become accustomed to the Australian way of life and culture.
>
> (A02, female, aged 61)

Thus, participants expressed the importance of family in maintaining a sense of home. Those who are without family members in the home country do not feel a sense of "returning home" when going back to their homeland, but, rather, they feel like a visitor or traveler. The participants' words further demonstrate the distinction between identification with the home culture and closeness to the home country. While a sense of cultural identity may remain, regardless of the ascribed identity that is sometimes incongruent with the cultural context, closeness to the country of origin might weaken once family members are no longer in the home country.

Transnational practice signifying home

The desire to keep close to Chinese co-ethnics in Australia motivates many older Chinese to choose to live in suburbs densely populated by residents of Chinese heritage. For one thing, ethnic enclaves provide a sense of home beyond the house and make life more convenient for those migrants who do not speak fluent English. Furthermore, various Asian or Chinese shops, supermarkets, restaurants, services, and Chinese community associations are more likely to be located close to or in locations with a concentration of residents of Chinese heritage. These resources facilitate transnational practices among Chinese co-ethnics, such as providing opportunities to participate in community activities that connect them to other Chinese in China and in Australia. Social engagement with co-ethnics can reduce isolation because friendship networks provide a sense of home in a foreign land. Several participants showed us photographs taken with friends at outings or gatherings, which highlighted to us the importance of maintaining social networks to older people's well-being. In addition, close proximity and easy access to Asian grocery stores allow them to purchase fruit, vegetables, food items, and everyday household items that they were familiar with back in China, which itself can bring back nostalgic feelings of the old home. One participant showed a photograph of a popular brand of potato crackers and explained how some food items can bring back her memory of those old days in China,

Photo 5.1 Popular Chinese potato crackers, branded Shang Hao Jia, are sold in an Asian supermarket in Brisbane, Australia.

Source: Shuang Liu. Used with permission.

84   *Home as a transnational place*

When I see the brands of food I was very familiar with in China in an Asian supermarket here, I think of my home country China and my life there in the past. I miss it very much. I remembered that I once saw packages of Shang Hao Jia potato crackers [a popular Chinese brand of snacks] on the shelves of a Chinese grocery store in Sunnybank [a Chinese-concentrated suburb in Brisbane]; I began to think of those old days in China. When my daughter was little then, I often bought these snacks for her – they were her favourite snacks.

(A20, female, aged 56)

This participant expressed her nostalgic feeling of her home country and old days. The quote illustrates that Asian supermarkets are not only places to buy familiar food or other items they used to get from home country, but also a transnational place where the old home and old self are extended into the new cultural context. Another participant who has lived in Australia for over a decade showed us a photograph taken at one of her gatherings with co-ethnics from her hometown. She expressed her nostalgia towards her former home in China by participating in social activities organised by co-ethnics from her hometown and wearing their association uniform to display belonging to China,

We moved to Australia more than a decade ago. We still miss China very much. China is our home. If China is strong and powerful, we feel proud. I wear this uniform of our town-mates association in Brisbane [pointing to the photograph]. I feel a strong sense of belonging to China when I wear it. I miss my hometown in China very much.

(B11, female, aged 65)

Several older Chinese participants expressed enjoyment in the opportunity to share their past experiences in their home country with Chinese friends of similar age because they have been through the same historical times in China and can understand and appreciate each other's feelings. These opportunities of sharing thoughts and feelings about their home country cannot be provided by their adult children who have not gone through the same life experiences as their parents.

The opportunity to share those experiences of old days with co-ethnics of the same generation can provide emotional comfort to older migrants. One type of space that facilitates such sharing of experiences is churches or temples. They are not only places for practising religious faith, but they just as importantly serve as a transnational social and cultural place for older Chinese to gather with friends, receive emotional support, and do things together to cherish their life in the old country, thereby extending the old

Home as a transnational place 85

self into the new cultural context. One participant described her experience this way,

> I regularly gather with my friends, for dinging out or drinking tea; we sometimes go to visit them in their house. We meet in the church every week, too. Such gatherings create opportunities for us to interact with each other and to keep us connected to what is going on around us.
>
> (A10, female, aged 66)

Participants feel strongly about the need to maintain old social connections back in China through mediated channels. All of them talk to their friends on the phone, via email or WhatsApp, and WeChat, albeit at different levels of frequency. One participant who has resided in Australia for 27 years described his reliance on communication technologies for keeping connected with friends and relatives,

> I use internet-enabled devices every day. I watch news from mobile phone and iPad, chat with friends and relatives using WhatsApp. I communicate with my best friends and relatives via email and WhatsApp and phone and other devices.
>
> (A04, male, aged 73)

The experiences of this participant in using the internet shows that, through transnational communication via the mediated channels, migrants are able to build, maintain, and reinforce multiple linkages with their country of origin and its people (Dunn, 2005). Regular and frequent contact with family and friends helps Chinese migrants to sustain cultural, social networks, and keep memories of China and a collective sense of Chineseness alive (Li & Chong, 2012).

In addition to strengthening transnational social relationships for migrants, communication technologies allow older migrants to access news and entertainment products from their home country through internet-enabled devices such as tablets, iPads, smartphones, and computers. Satellite TV allows them to watch TV soap operas from mainland China, Hong Kong, and Taiwan at the same time as the broadcasts occur in China. Some use internet technology to search for health-related information in the Chinese language. All these activities help to keep older Chinese migrants connected and engaged socially and culturally. International research suggests that social engagement is a prerequisite for quality of life and psychological well-being in old age (Yang, 2003). For example, findings based on the case of older Jewish immigrants from the Former Soviet Union in Israel show that using the internet for maintaining social networks helps elderly Jewish participants

Photo 5.2 An older Chinese couple use an iPad and smartphones to keep connected with friends back in China.
Source: Siqin Wang. Used with permission.

to cope with the distance from their loved ones, thereby improving their psychological well-being (Khvorostianov, Elias, & Nimrod, 2011). Delving into issues such as social and psychological well-being in transnational space provides a useful entry point for understanding the development of autobiographical insideness in the context of transnational communities. Transnational identity creation and practice provide a bridge between older Chinese migrants' past life in the home country and present life in the host country, fostering an emotional bond with both.

Conclusion

This chapter explores home as a transnational place and illustrates how older Chinese create and maintain a transnational community by extending their home culture into the host cultural context. The findings show that a Chinese migrant's home is a site where home and host cultures meet and where cultural identity is negotiated. Despite most of the older participants in the study self-identifying as Chinese-Australian, they perceive this hyphenated identity to be derived from different components of the two cultures. While the Australian component of their hyphenated identity is more likely to be associated with citizenship and a long period of residence in Australia, the Chinese component comes from something much deeper: beliefs, values, traditions, families, heritage, language, and ethnic physical appearances. The Chineseness is "in the blood". Similar to findings from a previous study on first, second, and 1.5 generation Chinese immigrants (Liu, 2015b), the current study on older Chinese immigrants provides support for the claim that identity and belonging to home and host cultures can be derived from different domains. Nevertheless, participants perceive that the Chinese and the Australian components of their cultural identity are compatible and even mutually reinforcing.

The findings show that language is an important component of the home-building process. All participants speak Chinese (Mandarin or Cantonese) at home. They want their grandchildren, often born in Australia, to be able to speak Chinese and carry on their heritage cultural traditions, highlighting the important role of language in preserving culture. As language is one of the main ways of communicating with groups and communities, the use of ethnic language signifies their membership to and identification with the Chinese diaspora community in Australia. In addition, practices that maintain transnational connections with home country China can preserve cultural continuity by linking the old self and the new self in the host country context. However, many older Chinese participants in our study do not feel they completely belong to either home or host cultures after migration. This can be due to change that has occurred in them as a process of acculturation, as well as change that has occurred in the old country, so, many decades later, neither the migrants nor their home country is as they were at the time of migrating. Nevertheless, the feeling of being a Chinese lives on in older Chinese migrants, no matter how long they have lived outside their homeland.

The acculturation literature (Berry, 2005) used to view home and host cultures as essentially at the opposite end of a continuum, and that an individual needs to abandon the heritage culture in order to be accepted as a fully competent member of the host culture. This view has long been

88 *Home as a transnational place*

replaced by an understanding that acceptance into the host culture is only a matter of degrees, and the two cultural domains are independent rather than at the opposite ends of the continuum. The participants in our study prefer to self-identify by a hyphenated identity to reflect that they are affiliated with both host and home cultures, albeit to a different degree of closeness. This hyphenated identity is relatively stable in heritage cultural values but may vary in salience, depending on the roles the individual plays in a particular social and cultural context. For example, sometimes they may more strongly identify as Chinese; and other times, they may more strongly identify as an Australian. However, our findings show that those multiple "selves" are not competing selves in those older Chinese migrants, as their home and host cultures are not in conflict, but are rather compatible, and even mutually reinforcing of each other.

Migration and transnationalism necessitate the reconsideration and reconstruction of cultural identity for migrants and transmigrants. Integration into the host cultural environment is an important part of migrants' acculturation in the host country. However, becoming part of the host culture does not come naturally or instantaneously for migrants upon arrival in the settlement country (Liu, 2015a). The simultaneous development of a sense of belonging to the host culture and the maintenance of attachment to the home culture can be a long and, at times, challenging process. Connectedness to either one's ethnic group or the larger cultural group is not merely affiliation between the self and the Other, but entails fundamental differences in the way through which the cultural identity is constructed in response to the cultural, social, and political environment in which one lives.

The findings in our study indicate that communication technologies play a key role in facilitating older migrants to keep connected with old social connections in the home country. Participants feel that, because they live in Australia, there is a need for them to maintain old friendships through mediated channels such as smartphones, social media such as WeChat (a Chinese social media platform), emails, and other internet-enabled platforms. However, geographical distance and an extended length of residence in the host country can weaken their sense of home in the old country. Some participants indicate that they do not have the feeling of "returning home" when they go back to visit their home country, either because old friends and family members are no longer there or because they no longer have a house as a symbol of home in their home country. These findings provide supports to the argument that the three dimensions of insideness (physical, social and cultural, and autobiographical) are not mutually exclusive (Rowles, 1983). Closely related to autobiographical insideness, or the emotional bond to a place developed from cumulative

Home as a transnational place 89

experiences of living in a place, is the key concept of physical insideness as well as social and cultural insideness, which together provide building blocks for a sense of home, identity, and belonging for older migrants ageing in a foreign land. The creation of identity through autobiographical insideness provides a continuity between the past and the present (Wahl & Oswald, 2010).

Settling into a new country is a complex process and acculturation is an ongoing, lifelong journey. For migrants, this journey always involves the negotiation of identity, belonging, and home that extends beyond geographic borders. While developing a cultural identity seems a natural process for people born and grown up in one place or one culture, for migrants who live and move between cultures, it is challenging to build a cultural identity in a transnational place because their "culture" is not associated with one place. Migrants constantly engage in striking a balance between the perception of their own ethnic identity and the perception of others' questioning of their ethnic heritage. When migrants move to the host country, the new cultural environment requires them to learn the national language (e.g., English) and to familiarise themselves with cultural practices of the host country. While integration into the host country gives them a sense of belonging there, distinct physical appearances remind them of "otherness". If identity negotiation involves coming to terms with the changing self, then which self becomes salient in what context is a function of an interaction between the characteristics of the person and the characteristics of the context. When home and host cultures coexist without merging, people may develop the ability to cross cultural boundaries and to move from one cultural milieu to another without feeling disoriented (Liu, 2015b). Those who can simultaneously navigate through home and host cultural frameworks and become skilled at adapting to situational characteristics achieve success in identity negotiation. The next chapter discusses implications for theories and practice in relation to home as a place, a set of relationships, and a transnational place, as well as identifying some directions for future research in ageing in a foreign land.

References

Ang, I. (2014). Beyond Chinese groupism: Chinese Australians between assimilation, multiculturalism and diaspora. *Ethnic and Racial Studies, 37*(7), 1184–1196.

Baldassar, L., Pyke, J., & Ben-Moshe, D. (2017). The Vietnamese in Australia: Diaspora identity, intra-group tensions, transnational ties and "victim" status. *Journal of Ethnic and Migration Studies, 43*(6), 937–955.

Bélanger, E., & Verkuyten, M. (2010). Hyphenated identities and acculturation: Second-generation Chinese of Canada and the Netherlands. *Identity: An International Journal of Theory and Research, 10*(3), 141–163.

90 Home as a transnational place

Berry, J. W. (2005). Acculturation: Living successfully in two cultures. *International Journal of Intercultural Relations, 29*, 697–712.

Brockhall, F., & Liu, S. (2011). Performing new Australians: Identity (re)construction of long-term Greek and Cypriot immigrants in Australia. *China Media Research, 7*(1), 16–24.

Clifford, J. (1994). Diasporas. *Cultural Anthropology, 9*(3), 302–338.

Clifford, J. (1997). *Routes: Travel and translation in the late twentieth century.* Cambridge, MA: Harvard University Press.

Cohen, R. (2008). *Global diasporas: An introduction.* London and New York: Routledge.

Dunn, K. M. (2005). A paradigm of transnationalism for migration studies. *New Zealand Population Review, 31*(2), 15–31.

Goffman, E. (1969). *The presentation of self in everyday life.* London: Penguin Books.

Green, A. E., Power, M. R., & Jang, D. M. (2008). Trans-Tasman migration: New Zealanders' explanations for their move. *New Zealand Geographer, 64*, 34–45.

Hall, S. (1990). Cultural identity and diaspora. In J. Rutherford (Ed.), *Identity, community, culture, difference* (pp. 222–237). London: Lawrence & Wishart.

Hecht, M., Warren, J. R., Jung, E., & Krieger, J. L. (2005). The communication theory of identity. In W. B. Gudykunst (Ed.), *Theorizing about intercultural communication* (pp. 257–278). Thousand Oaks, CA: Sage.

Huang, Y. (2011). Identity negotiation in relation to context of communication. *Theory and Practice in Language Studies, 1*, 219–225.

Khvorostianov, N., Elias, N., & Nimrod, G. (2011). "Without it I am nothing": The internet in the lives of older immigrants. *New Media & Society, 14*(4), 583–599.

Kim, Y. Y. (1994). Beyond cultural identity. *Intercultural Communication Studies, 4*, 1–25.

Li, W. W., & Chong, M. D. (2012). Transnationalism, social wellbeing and older Chinese migrants. *Graduate Journal of Asia Pacific Studies, 8*(1), 29–44.

Lim, S. S., Bork-Hüffer, T., & Yeoh, B. S. A. (2016). Mobility, migration, and new media: Manoeuvring through physical, digital and liminal spaces. *New Media & Society, 18*(10), 2147–2154.

Liu, S. (2015a). *Identity, hybridity and cultural home: Chinese migrants and diaspora in multicultural societies.* London: Rowman & Littlefield International.

Liu, S. (2015b). In search for a sense of place: Identity negotiation of Chinese immigrants. *International Journal of Intercultural Relations, 46*, 26–35.

Markus, H., & Nurius, P. (1986). Possible selves. *American Psychologist, 41*, 954–969.

Mead, G. H. (1934). *Mind, self and society from the standpoint of a social behaviorist.* Chicago, IL: Chicago University Press.

Portes, A. (1997). Immigration theory for a new century: Some problems and opportunities. *International Migration Review, 31*(4), 799–852.

Rowles, G. D. (1983). Place and personal identity in old age: Observations from Appalachia. *Journal of Environmental Psychology, 3*, 299–313.

Home as a transnational place 91

Siu, L. (2005). Queen of the Chinese colony: Gender, nation, and belonging in diaspora. *Anthropological Quarterly*, *78*(3), 511–542.

Tajfel, H., & Turner, J. (1979). An integrative theory of intergroup conflict. In W. G. Austin & S. Worchel (Eds.), *The social psychology of intergroup relations* (pp. 33–47). Monterey, CA: Brooks/Cole.

Tan, C-B. (2013). Introduction. In C-B. Tan (Ed.), *Routledge handbook of the Chinese diaspora*. (pp. 1–12). New York and London: Routledge.

Ting-Toomey, S. (2005). Identity negotiation theory: Crossing cultural boundaries. In W. B. Gudykunst (Ed.), *Theorizing about intercultural communication* (pp. 211–233). Thousand Oaks, CA: Sage.

Wahl, N-W., & Oswald, F. (2010). Environmental perspectives on ageing. In D. Dannefer & C. Phillipson (Eds.), *The Sage handbook of social gerontology* (pp. 111–124). London: Sage.

Yang, G. (2003). The internet and the rise of transnational Chinese cultural sphere. *Media, Culture & Society*, *25*, 469–490.

6 Building a sense of home in a foreign land

Introduction

Building a sense of home in a foreign land is an ongoing process for Chinese migrants in particular, as well as for migrants of other cultural backgrounds in general. This sense of home is embedded in the transnational space they navigate in everyday routines as their life straddles their country of origin and country of settlement. On the one hand, living in-between cultures can lead to positive outcomes for migrants, such as the development of intercultural competencies to switch between cultures in response to situational requirements. On the other hand, such bicultural exposures can make some migrants feel that they belong only peripherally to both home and host cultures. Because culture is not associated with one place for migrants, they continuously negotiate their sense of home between the old and the new countries, and thus forge novel configurations of identification with home in both places. Home for migrants is multidimensional, incorporating physical, social, cultural, material, and emotional domains. It is important for researchers, therefore, to delve into the dynamic ways in which migrants continue to shape their person-environment relationships through developing familiarity with the physical environment (physical insideness), social and cultural connections (social and cultural insideness), as well as identity and belonging (autobiographical insideness) in the new country. These three types of insideness, as proposed by Rowles (1983), are interconnected. Familiarity with the physical environment will give migrants the confidence to get out of their house, and will encourage social participation. Active social engagement, in turn, will further build familiarity with and confidence in navigating the local environment. Environmental and social and cultural connectedness can collectively cultivate a strong sense of identity and belonging to the place, thereby contributing to well-being in older migrants.

This concluding chapter furthers the discussion of ageing in a foreign land by exploring implications for theory and practice. Using concepts

Building a sense of home in a foreign land   93

of home and cultural home, the chapter first delineates the relationship between identity and belonging in a transnational space. The empirical data from older Chinese migrants presented in previous chapters illustrate that family and social relationships extending into the homeland are central to building a sense of home for older migrants. It is through navigating these webs of relationships within and beyond geographical borders that older migrants develop attachment to place, negotiate cultural identities, maintain transnational social and cultural connections, and build both a physical and symbolic sense of home in Australia. This chapter challenges the conventional notions of integration and biculturalism in acculturation theories, and contributes a transnational perspective to environmental gerontology. In addition, the chapter draws implication for practices regarding providing culturally appropriate social support to assist older migrants to age well in a foreign land. We argue that building a sense of home away from one's homeland involves an older migrant's capacity to reintegrate with place and people in the context of transnational space. The chapter concludes by identifying some directions for further research to delve into the dynamic ways in which older migrants build a sense of home beyond locality and culture.

Home beyond locality and culture

Home has been studied from the perspectives of both the instrumental approach and the affective approach. The former views home as a physical and geographical location of a dwelling place, whereas the latter views home more as a socially constructed place with emotional, personal, cultural, and social significance to dwellers. The affective approach, which is the most relevant to this book, conceptualises home as a symbolic expression of the self that is often understood in relation to the larger context of identity, belonging, and culture (Seo & Mazumdar, 2011). The social and cultural significance of home environments and the relationship of home to identity and belonging have received increased attention from researchers in the field of acculturation and ageing because, ultimately, "home is where we belong" (Chaudhury & Rowles, 2005, p. 3). Situating the concept of home in the social and cultural context broadens its domain to communities. To identify as a member of a particular ethnic or cultural community and to be accepted by the cultural group, an individual needs to learn the shared norms and rules that govern behaviours of the ingroup. People who are in cultural transition, such as migrants, face the challenge of learning a new set of cultural rules and reconciling differences between home and host cultures. While cultural knowledge cannot be reduced to cognitive content (Markus & Kitayama, 2003), it is nevertheless ingrained into an individual's

94 *Building a sense of home in a foreign land*

sense of being. Identification with a cultural group suggests that the individual shares part of his or her being with members of that culture. A migrant's home, by extension, is a cultural home. The concept of cultural home, proposed by Vivero and Jenkins (1999), is often used together with ethnic enclaves to refer to a sense of belonging to an ethnic or cultural community that provides members with a sense of solidarity because similarity in heritage culture creates symbolic and emotional ties among members. First-generation older Chinese migrants in Australia, for example, bring with them significant attachments to their heritage culture. Cultural transition always involves some feeling of discontinuity of identity and culture. When those older Chinese migrants interact with co-ethnics in their ethnic community, their Chinese identity is reinforced through adherence to their heritage cultural traditions and the use of Chinese language. The development of an ethnic identity, regardless of one's ethnicity, provides the individual with a historical continuity based on a common cultural heritage (Smith, 1991). A cultural home thus enables people who undergo cultural transition to find a sense of grounding through emotional attachment to their cultural group (Navarrete & Jenkins, 2011). Consequently, cultural home communicates to migrants not only the concept of location and place, but also identity, belonging, and continuity of their heritage culture.

However, the extent to which migrants can identify with and be accepted as a full cultural member of the receiving country depends, at least partially, on the social, political, and cultural environment of the larger society. For example, the policy of Anglo-conformity in post–World War II Australia demanded immigrants' complete renunciation of their ethnic culture to assimilate into the behaviour and values of the White Australia majority, thus meeting the imposed societal expectations to become "new Australians". The expectation was that there would be as little difference as possible between immigrants and the Anglo-Australians, at least culturally (Bottomley, 1979). Similarly in the United States, the Chinese migrant group historically was singled out for legal exclusion on the basis of race (Zhou, 2014), being barred from naturalisation and assimilation by the Chinese Exclusion Act (1992–1943). Before World War II, Chinese migrants were forced to take refuge in Chinatowns, and depended on ethnic economies and institutions for survival. Even after Congress repealed the Chinese Exclusion Act in 1943, most Chinese immigrants remained isolated in ethnic enclaves and refrained from participating in mainstream American life.

The implementation of multicultural policies in many immigrant-receiving countries and the abolition of various immigration restriction acts have changed the political, social, and cultural landscape for modern-day immigrants. As such, modern-day immigration is very different from earlier waves of migration, which consisted of images of permanent displacement,

Building a sense of home in a foreign land 95

a complete break from one's homeland, and a hard transition to a new language, life, and land (Glick Schiller, Basch, & Blanc, 1995). Contemporary migrants travel between their country of origin and country of settlement, inhibit multiple homes, perform different roles, and speak more than one language. Unlike their predecessors in the United States and Australia in the 1800s whose migration journey involved a move away from home culture followed by enforced assimilation, modern-day Chinese migrants, particularly transnational migrants, construct bicultural or multicultural identities, create social networks in both cultures, and continue cultural practices that exist in the country of origin into the country of settlement, instead of being pressured to assimilate into the mainstream culture. These changes feed into debates about transitions from Chinese ethnic identity to hyphenated identities that reflect new forms of identification.

With increasing border-crossing movements of migrants and transmigrants, cultural home is increasingly marked by symbolic rather than geographical territories. We cannot simply map out a culture with a place. For migrants or transmigrants whose life straddles two cultures, cultural borders have become increasingly more permeable; so too are the boundaries of their cultural identities. The traditional belief among social scientists that identity boundaries are something everyone both experiences, and ought to feel reluctant to change or compromise (Kim, 2008) has been replaced by the view that identity is fluid, never fixed, and a product of social construction (Ting-Toomey, 2005). Consequently, a migrant's sense of home, in its broad sense, is beyond one locality and one culture. However, moving between cultures is not simply about speaking different languages to meet situational or cultural requirements, but rather, a process entailing the negotiation of dynamic cultural identity in social interactions. Identity is a product of social construction; so is a culture home.

Implications for theory

Identity and belonging have been central to acculturation research for more than five decades. Regardless of the reasons for migrating, acculturation is a process all migrants undergo in their host countries. Although acculturation is also experienced by host nationals in the immigrant-receiving country, this book focuses on the acculturation experiences of migrants. While migrants' acculturation can occur at different levels, it is, at its most basic level, about identity – who we are and how we relate to others. Systematic investigations of cultural identity can be traced back to psychologist Erik Erikson (1968) who places identity at the core of the individual and his or her culture, and views the process of identity development as a process of merging the personal and cultural identities into a coherent whole. Berry's

96 *Building a sense of home in a foreign land*

(2005) model of acculturation from the perspective of cross-cultural psychology proposes that acculturation provides the means for which one's home culture and identity, and that of the host culture, can be integrated in a bicultural identity. The state of biculturalism is sometimes equated with integration, which refers to migrants' maintenance of the heritage culture while maintaining participation in the host culture (Ward, 2008). Acculturation scholars have made various attempts to understand bicultural identities. Notably, the concept of Bicultural Identity Integration (BII; Benet-Martinez & Haritatos, 2005) seeks to capture the extent to which bicultural individuals perceive their home and host cultural identities (e.g., Chinese and American) as compatible and integrated (high BII) versus oppositional and separate (low BII). However, findings are mixed with regard to the benefits of bicultural identity. Some researchers argue that integrating two or more cultures in one identity leads to greater benefits than choosing to identify with a single culture. Others believe that the process of dealing with more than one culture and acquiring more than one behavioural repertoire can cause stress, isolation, and identity confusion. These mixed findings cannot be easily reconciled using existing theoretical models such as BII and other frameworks of bicultural identity. One key reason is that while those models may be used to measure migrants' perceived distance or compatibility between old and new cultures, they cannot explain the process through which distinctive cultural identities of migrants are negotiated and reconciled to maintain balance in identity and belonging as they live in the host country.

This knowledge gap is filled, to some extent, by our research on older Chinese migrants. As processed-oriented qualitative studies, our research advances an understanding of how cultural identities are negotiated during acculturation processes. The hyphenated identity most participants develop, Chinese-Australian, represents their dual cultural affiliation. In the case of older Chinese migrants, they call Australia home and see themselves as Australians, at least partially, while they simultaneously feel set apart from the mainstream Anglo-Australians by their Chinese physical appearances, language, and ethnic culture. Consequently, the dual cultural components in their hyphenated identity co-exist without merging into one another, although elements of the two cultures are not incompatible. Communicating with co-ethnics evokes among those older Chinese their sense of belonging and desire to maintain their Chineseness, and being with family members in Australia and Australian citizenship status make them feel Australian. What our research findings suggest is that a hyphenated cultural identity does not necessarily mean equal identification with both cultures. Moreover, not everyone living in the bicultural environment such as migrants will function as a bicultural just because the environment is such. People can be exposed

Building a sense of home in a foreign land 97

to two cultures but still engage in monocultural communication, as most older Chinese participants in our studies did. This argument supports Phinney and Devich-Navarro's (1997) distinction of two types of biculturalism. The first is blended biculturalism, which refers to integrating the heritage and host cultures into a new, unique bicultural identity that is not directly reducible to either the heritage or the host culture. The second one is shifted biculturalism, which refers to shifting behaviours to be consistent with the cultural context. Both types of biculturalism are practised among migrants, as Phinney and Devich-Navarro (1997, p. 19) pointed out, "there is not just one way of being bicultural". However, our findings show that those older Chinese migrants, who indicate their dual cultural affiliations, prefer shifting biculturalism.

Biculturalism is an integral part of acculturation processes, and is deemed to be the state of integration (Nguyen & Benet-Martinez, 2007). Acculturation literature has consistently identified integration orientation (as compared to assimilation, separation, and marginalisation) as most preferred by both immigrants and host nationals (Ward, 2008). Immigrants who prefer integration are more likely to develop biculturalism, as they endorse both their culture of origin and the mainstream culture of the receiving country (Berry & Sam, 1997). However, it needs to be noted, though, that biculturalism has not always emerged as the most adaptive approach to immigrant acculturation (Schwartz & Unger, 2010). An international meta-analysis based on 83 studies and over 23,000 participants shows that findings are mixed with regard to the direction and magnitude of the association between integration (biculturalism) and acculturation outcomes (Nguyen & Benet-Martinez, 2013). This boils down to the question of when biculturalism is adaptive. Research evidence shows that biculturalism is most adaptive in a bicultural environment where being able to navigate within more than one culture provides a distinct advantage (Schwartz & Zamboanga, 2008). On the other hand, being bicultural could be a disadvantage in monocultural contexts, due to discrepancies between self-claimed identity and ascribed identity. This argument is supported by the findings from older Chinese migrants in our studies; some of them encountered identity incongruences when they visited China because their fellow Chinese regarded them as Australians, rather than Chinese. These findings suggest that if the context is monocultural, it may be more adaptive for a bicultural individual to behave and think in ways that are more consistent with that culture.

Our research contributes to theories of environmental gerontology by bringing in a transnational perspective. Theorising of environmental gerontology was not originally intended to apply to understand the person-environment relationships among migrants (Wahl & Oswald, 2010). However, application of this theory to understand the home-building

98 *Building a sense of home in a foreign land*

experiences of Chinese migrants enriches both fields of acculturation and environmental gerontology. Contemporary migrants are transnational as they "forge and sustain simultaneous multi-stranded social relations that link together their societies of origin and settlement" (Glick Schiller et al., 1995, p. 48). Viewed from the transnational perspective, the three dimensions of insideness represent complementary aspects of the process of building a sense of home in a foreign land, although the three insideness dimensions may not necessarily develop at the same speed or in a linear fashion. Older migrants may be able to establish familiarity with the new physical environment after settling in the country for a period of time, then subsequently rebuild new social networks and reconnect with old networks in their country of origin. The new social networks would encourage social engagement and participation, even in activities only involved co-ethnics. Social participation, in turn, would further develop confidence and competence in older migrants to navigate the physical environment in which they live. Identity, belonging, and emotional bond to a place or autobiographical insideness both reinforce and are reinforced by both sociocultural connectedness and familiarity with the environment. In addition, as observed by Rowles (1983), identity, belonging, and emotional bond to a place may be developed through material objects with emotional meanings, such as a painting by an old friend from the home country. Some participants described how they used Chinese decorations in the house and furniture shipped from China to create a sense of home. These material objects are reminiscent of the old self and extend it into the new environment, thereby preserving identity continuity. The processes through which the three dimensions of insideness develop and interact with one another shed light on our understanding of the transnational nature of the meaning of home and place for older people ageing in a foreign land.

The findings from our research on older Chinese migrants highlight the importance of people in building a sense of home and belonging. While communication technologies allow them to keep connected with old social ties in the home country, geographic distance and extended length of stay in the host country can weaken their sense of home in the old country. Some participants indicated that they did not have the feeling of "returning home" when they went back to visit their home country either because old friends and family members were no longer there or because the home country had changed much since they left. Underlying emotional bond to a place is the key concept of family and social relationships, which provides the building blocks for a sense of home, identity, and belonging. As Wiles and colleagues (2012, p. 358) state, building a sense of place is "not merely about attachment to a particular home but where the older person is continually reintegrating with places and renegotiating meanings and identity

Building a sense of home in a foreign land 99

in the face of dynamic landscapes of social, political, cultural, and personal change". It is this subjective feeling of belonging that contributes to older migrants' place attachment, place identity, and a sense of home.

Implications for practice

Our research findings show that older Chinese prefer a hyphenated cultural identity. However, such bicultural identity may not necessarily equate to a strong sense of cultural identification with both cultures. Moreover, the Chinese and the Australian components of their hyphenated identity tend to be derived from different domains, with the Chineseness more likely to reside "in the blood" and the Australianness more likely to relate to citizenship and long-term residence in the host country. Further, the sense of being accepted into the mainstream cultural group might not always translate into a sense of belonging to that group because ethnic physical appearances and cultural traditions may still set them apart. These findings can inform the design of training programs by community and government settlement services for migrants. Current settlement training programs tend to emphasise learning the language of the host country, familiarisation with national cultural norms, and integration into the larger society. Future training programs may incorporate an understanding of the separate components and functions of ethnic and national identities, and focus more on compatibility and coexistence of ethnic and national cultures, accepting that integration does not necessarily mean the merging of two cultures. Utilising ethnic cultural identification to facilitate integration into the larger society may help to build confidence and competence in migrants to navigate through the two cultures.

Our research generates insight into what resources older Chinese migrants draw on to build a sense of home in a foreign land. One significant finding is that many participants constructed a sense of home in green spaces, predominantly the private gardens in their home. Existing literature in gerontology explores the role of green spaces in nursing homes or retirement villages. For example, Raske (2010) found that gardens play an immensely positive role in the lives of older residents in nursing homes because the garden is a place where residents connect with each other and engage in meaningful activities, thereby enhancing life satisfaction. There is little research, however, that explores the social and cultural significance of private gardens in creating a sense of home, particularly for migrants who face the challenge of rebuilding home in a foreign land. Since the findings from our research suggest that gardens play an important role for older Chinese migrants to link their old home in the homeland to their new home in a foreign land, there is a need for aged care providers to explore the social and cultural

100 *Building a sense of home in a foreign land*

potential of gardens in improving older people's ageing experiences. For example, at the community level, we tend to see established gardens maintained by professional gardeners in many residential areas, apartment complexes, or nursing homes. What we rarely find is a patch of land or bare garden space, allowing older residents in the neighbourhood to put their own footprint in them. Future practice may consider the creation of community gardens in neighbourhoods where there is a concentration of older migrants. Such garden spaces can function as an enabling social and physical place for older migrants to plant vegetables and plants reminiscent of their old home in their country of origin. The process of creating a green space of their own can enable older people to connect, participate in physical activities, and remember their homelands by growing vegetables and plants that can be used for their cultural dishes. Such practice can help to continue the old self into the new country, thereby preserving a sense of cultural continuity.

Our research on older Chinese participants highlight the importance of physical cultural objects, and how these material objects can provide a link to their home culture. This finding has implications for aged care providers, such as community care providers. Objects reminiscent of home culture can be used by care professionals to foster deeper relationships with older clients, and to engage them in story-telling to learn more about their experiences and provide more culturally appropriate care. Community care providers may organise trips to ethnic markets or supermarkets; the experience of purchasing familiar products from home country can be psychologically and emotionally rewarding. In addition, many community care associations run regular social activities for older migrants. The design of programs may incorporate asking clients to bring a cultural object or an object with emotional attachment, and to share their stories with fellow clients. Recollection of meaningful objects associated with a sense of home or socially shared reminiscence evoked by cultural objects can provide continuity of the old self into the new cultural context (Burr & Butt, 2000).

Our research findings consistently show the importance of social participation and social connectedness in well-being for older Chinese migrants. Social connectedness revolves around relationships and being in contact with other people (Nayar & Wright-StClair, 2018). Older Chinese migrants' involvement in regular social and community activities provide them with opportunities for contact outside the home, emotional support and the exchange of information, helping to improve their quality of life (Li & Chong, 2012). Older migrants are more likely to be linguistically isolated and depend on their children to communicate with people outside their community (Trang, 2008), hindering social participation. Regular social activities organised by community care associations for older migrants from the

Photo 6.1 Cathay Community Association, established in 1984, specialises in supporting older Asian migrants, mostly of Chinese heritage, to settle into a new life in Australia through regular respite social activities and home care services.
Source: Shuang Liu. Used with permission.

same cultural backgrounds, along with transportation services, can provide opportunities to reconnect with co-ethnics of same age group and culture. Participants in our study expressed that sharing experiences with co-ethnics of the same age group can have benefits that talking with family members might not be able to offer. In addition, being greeted by neighbours can foster a sense of belonging and security derived from familiarity with the local community. The friendships, access to resources, and familiar environments can make older people feel attached to their communities as insiders (Wiles, Leibing, Guberman, Reeve, & Allen, 2012). Our findings further support previous research by reinforcing that social interactions with others, even those who are not close network members, can have the power to positively influence well-being (Sandstrom & Dunn, 2014). The implication for practice is that community associations may organise social activities involving neighbours to extend the sense of home beyond the house into the local

102 *Building a sense of home in a foreign land*

communities. Such a practice can also expand the base of social support for older people in their neighbourhood and communities.

Directions for further research

Many first-generation older Chinese migrants have resided in the host country for several decades. However, there have been relatively few longitudinal studies of older Chinese acculturation over time to capture acculturative change over time, compared with that of younger generations who are deemed more easily adapted to change resulting from cultural transition. Acculturation is a dynamic, complex, and multi-faceted process, longitudinal research will help illuminate long-term effects of integration in predicting successful acculturation outcomes. In addition, although Chinese diaspora communities have been among the most studied immigrant groups in the acculturation literature, most of the studies have relied on the assumption that acculturation is a universal process (Ward & Lin, 2010). There is little consideration of culture-specific dynamics of Chinese acculturation and adaptation processes. It is worthy of further research to explore whether there is anything unique about Chinese acculturation. Further, to date, we know a lot about acculturation attitudes and outcomes, but we know considerably less about the processes through which migrants achieve desired acculturation outcomes. The process aspect is largely under-investigated in acculturation research (Ward, 2008). Future research in acculturation needs to shift the traditional focus from assessing attitudes and outcomes to delineating the essential qualities and core processes of identity negotiation, particularly in a transnational space. Understanding the processes through which older Chinese migrants negotiate cultural meanings within themselves as they build a sense of home in a foreign land can inform both theory and practice in relation to ageing migrants.

Identity is at the core of acculturation. Existing acculturation models largely explain identity and group membership in terms of dualities; i.e., we define what and who we are vis-à-vis what and who we are not (Tajfel & Turner, 1979). Contemporary multicultural society is very different from what it was 50 years ago when the dominant acculturation models were developed on the assumption that acculturation involved a small number of migrants who needed to adapt to a monolithic national culture. In an era of increasing transmigration and border crossing, identity becomes multi-layered. We define our own identities and that of others within the realm of interdependent and interconnected networks of culture and people. Moreover, the social and economic composition (e.g., education, occupation, income) of the Chinese migrant population in particular (and migrants in general) and their mobility today are very different from what

Building a sense of home in a foreign land 103

they were decades ago. It is important for future research to explore the process through which modern-day Chinese migrants achieve integration in a society already influenced by waves of multi-ethnic migrants over several generations. Immigrants' choice of cultural identities relate to social cohesion in important ways because the social (cultural) group from which they derive those identities shapes their sense of belonging and how they relate to others in intergroup and interethnic situations.

Much research on identity and cultural home has been directed towards understanding the acculturation experiences of immigrant youths and second generation migrants (e.g., Berry, Phinney, Sam, & Vedder, 2006). However, relatively little attention has been paid to understanding the older migrant generation, and how they negotiate identity and locate a cultural home in a myriad of bicultural and intergenerational differences (Liu, 2015). Literature documents that immigration to a new culture at an older age gives rise to experiences of biographical disruption and status-discrepancy, which may invoke isolation, anxiety, and a sense of dislocation and loss (Li & Chong, 2012). For example, older Asian immigrants in Canada have been reported to experience cultural incompatibility, barriers to accessing service, and exclusion, all of which subsequently affects their psychological well-being (Lai & Surood, 2013). Due to cultural norms, older Chinese migrants are often reluctant to access social support from professional services or formal care for fear it would be considered as family rejection. Despite the prevalence of social isolation and language barriers among older migrants, we have limited knowledge of how they deal with both acculturation and ageing in a foreign land. Increasingly, government policies encourage older people to age in place, that is, older people living in their own home for as long as possible with the right support in place. The question of how ageing migrants, family, community, and the larger society can collectively help older migrants to build a sense of home, identity, and belonging to overcome social isolation and facilitate access to culturally appropriate services warrants further research.

We live in an interconnected world, thanks to communication technologies. As an integral part of our lives, communication technologies deterritorialise social networks by connecting older migrants in a transnational space, linking their country of origin with their country of settlement. The widespread use of internet-enabled devices and platforms, such as social media, WeChat, Facebook, emails, and smartphones, have given rise to new ways of developing and maintaining social relationships. The internet also enables older migrants to search, post, share, and receive information about each other, the home country, and the host country. Therefore, the advancement in communication technologies and, in particular, the evolution of social media facilitate the processes of transnationalism and provide older

104 *Building a sense of home in a foreign land*

migrants with immediate, frequent, and continuous engagement with the homeland (Baldassar, Pyke, & Ben-Moshe, 2017). Li and Chong's (2012) study found that older Chinese migrants in New Zealand travelled to China to have a health check-up or to see a Chinese doctor who speaks their ethnic language. Future research may explore the potential of using communication technologies to deliver health-related information, including allowing older migrants to access professional health services in their own language or even from their home country.

Conclusion

This book advances a new understanding of acculturation processes for older migrants, drawing on empirical data from migrants of Chinese heritage in Australia. Drawing on insights from environmental gerontology, intercultural communication, and acculturation theories, this book conceptualises ageing in a foreign land as a home-building process, highlighting the collective contributions of individual, community, social, cultural, technological, and environmental factors to older migrants' well-being. Special consideration is given to what it means to age "in place" for those whose home is not necessarily attached to one place and one culture. We argue that building a sense of home in a foreign land is not just about developing attachment to a particular home as a physical location; more importantly, it involves an older migrant's capacity to continually reintegrate with place and people in the context of change in personal, social, cultural, and physical environments.

Home forms the basis for the development of identity and nurtures a feeling of belonging. When migrants relocate into a new culture, the sense of identity and belonging has to be negotiated in the new context because cultural transition brings with it the loss of social networks, family connections, social status, comfort, trust, independence, and even income. Consequently, migrants initially feel "out of place" and have to rebuild a sense of home to which they belong. Thus, the development of a sense of belonging is a key part of the acculturation process. Home recognises the significance of social identification in the construction and maintenance of place (Chaudhury & Rowles, 2005). Indeed, home and place are fundamental to older people developing their person-environmental relationship in a new country. The meaning of home for migrants is not only a product of individual, social, and cultural experience within the host country, but also of the experience of place and people going back to the country of origin.

A migrant's home is a site where heritage culture is preserved, practised, and passed on from generation to generation. For more than 200 years, Chinese migrants have endeavoured to maintain their culture, language, and

Building a sense of home in a foreign land 105

traditions in foreign lands, while adapting and adjusting to the local conditions of their receiving countries. The continuity of Chinese culture is seen in generations of migrants with Chinese ancestry, no matter which parts of the world they choose to call home. For older Chinese, cross-cultural adaptation into the host society is always accompanied by passing on cultural traditions to younger generations. The burgeoning number of Chinese language schools for locally born children of Chinese migrants and the various ethnic Chinese media play an important role in transmitting Chinese culture and maintaining Chinese cultural identity. Identity is a matter of positioning, as Stuart Hall (2003) pointed out. Thus, as the Chinese immigrants are positioning themselves in the new cultural space, they create space for their cultural home.

Building a sense of home in a foreign land is an ongoing process for older Chinese immigrants, as well as for migrants from other culturally and linguistically diverse backgrounds. This sense of home and belonging is embedded in the bicultural context they navigate through in their everyday lives. Living in-between cultures could make them feel they belong peripherally to both home and host cultures; on the other hand, such bicultural experiences could lead to positive outcomes such as the development of intercultural competencies to switch between cultures. Because "culture" is not associated with one place, immigrants continuously negotiate their sense of home between the old and the new worlds and thus forge novel configurations of identification with home in both places as they become more familiar with the once unfamiliar host country. As the concept of "home" is multidimensional, ranging from psychological to physical aspects, it is important for acculturation researchers to delve into the dynamic ways in which immigrants continue to locate a sense of home as their life strides across home and host countries. Process-oriented research is needed in order to better account for the range of outcomes associated with integration and biculturalism.

Our research identified ways in which older Chinese migrants assigned meanings to home, identity, and belonging in Australia. Such research enriches our understanding of how home is experienced both as a location and as a set of relationships among older immigrants ageing in a foreign land. For most migrants living in contemporary diaspora, negotiation with two cultures is fluid. In this sense, integration may be achieved only temporarily, lost at some stages of the process and then achieved again. Therefore, the identity negotiation process is ongoing, and multiple identities do not necessarily lead to identity conflict. The question is balance. Ting-Toomey (2005, p. 230) compares identity negotiation to ice-skating, describing a dynamic ice skater as someone "who can maintain an optimal sense of balance and grace as she or he waltzes through the maze of identity chaos

106 *Building a sense of home in a foreign land*

and the identity discovery process". Research on Chinese immigrants' cultural identity negotiation has to "waltz through" the complex relationship between cultures and identities to enhance our understanding of the nature of bicultural identities and to draw implications for "ice-skaters" in relation to how to strike an optimal balance between cultures.

This concluding chapter aims to mark the beginning of new discussions on ageing in a foreign land, and to function as an impetus to inspire further research on identity and cultural home. Given increasing global interconnectivity and the emergence of transnational diaspora, we can no longer consider home, culture, ethnicity, or race as contained within a geographic locale. This book challenges the traditional models of acculturation, questions the conventional notion of integration as well as analyses the fluid nature of cultural identities. As government policies worldwide encourage older people to age "in place", that is, to live independently for as long as possible in their own home, further research is needed to delve into the dynamic ways in which older migrants engage in building a sense of home beyond locality and culture.

References

Baldassar, L., Pyke, J., & Ben-Moshe, D. (2017). The Vietnamese in Australia: Diaspora identity, intra-group tensions, transnational ties and "victim" status. *Journal of Ethnic and Migration Studies, 43*(6), 937–955.

Benet-Martínez, V., & Haritatos, J. (2005). Bicultural Identity Integration (BII): Components and psychological antecedents. *Journal of Personality, 73,* 1015–1050.

Berry, J. W. (2005). Acculturation: Living successfully in two cultures. *International Journal of Intercultural Relations, 29,* 697–712.

Berry, J. W., Phinney, J. S., Sam, D. L., & Vedder, P. (2006). Immigrant youth: Acculturation, identity, and adaptation. *Applied Psychology, 55*(3), 303–332.

Berry, J. W., & Sam, D. L. (1997). Acculturation and adaptation. In J. W. Berry, M. H. Segall, & C. Kagitcibasi (Eds.), *Handbook of cross-cultural psychology* (Vol. 3, pp. 291–236). Boston, MA: Allyn & Bacon.

Bottomley, G. (1979). *After the Odyssey: A study of Greek Australians.* Brisbane: University of Queensland Press.

Burr, V., & Butt, T. (2000). Psychological distress and postmodern thought. In D. Fee (Ed.), *Pathology and postmodern: Mental illness as discourse and experience* (pp. 116–140). London: Sage.

Chaudhury, H., & Rowles, G. D. (2005). Between the shores of recollection and imagination: Self, aging, and home. In G. D. Rowles & H. Chaudhury (Eds.), *Home and identity in late life: International perspectives* (pp. 3–18). New York, NY: Springer.

Erikson, E. (1968). Identity, psychological. In W. A. Darity Jr. (Ed.), *International encyclopaedia of the social sciences* (pp. 46–48). New York, NY: Macmillan.

Building a sense of home in a foreign land 107

Glick Schiller, N., Basch, L., & Blanc, C. S. (1995). From immigrant to transmigrant: Theorizing transnational migration. *Anthropological Quarterly, 68*, 48–63.

Hall, S. (2003). Cultural identity and diaspora. In J. E. Braziel & A. Mannur (Eds.), *Theorizing diaspora: A reader* (pp. 233–246). Malden, MA: Blackwell Publishing.

Kim, Y. Y. (2008). Intercultural personhood: Globalization and a way of being. *International Journal of Intercultural Relations, 32*, 359–368.

Lai, D. W. L., & Surood, S. (2013). Effect of service barriers on health status of aging South Asian immigrants in Calgary, Canada. *Health & Social Work, 38*(1), 41–50.

Li, W. W., & Chong, M. D. (2012). Transnationalism, social wellbeing and older Chinese migrants. *Graduate Journal of Asia Pacific Studies, 8*(1), 29–44.

Liu, S. (2015). *Identity, hybridity and cultural home: Chinese migrants and diaspora in multicultural societies.* London: Rowman & Littlefield International.

Markus, H., & Kitayama, S. (2003). Culture, self, and the reality of the social. *Psychological Inquiry, 14*, 277–283.

Navarrete, V., & Jenkins, S. R. (2011). Cultural homelessness, multiminority status, ethnic identity development, and self esteem. *International Journal of Intercultural Relations, 35*, 791–804.

Nayar, S., & Wright-St Clair, W. A. (2018). Strengthening community: Older Asian immigrants' contributions to New Zealand society. *Journal of Cross-Cultural Gerontology, 33*, 355–368.

Nguyen, A-M. T. D., & Benet-Martinez, V. (2007). Biculturalism unpacked: Components, measurement, individual differences, and outcomes. *Social and Personality Psychology Compass, 1*, 101–114.

Nguyen, A-M. T. D., & Benet-Martinez, V. (2013). Biculturalism and adjustment: A meta-analysis. *Journal of Cross-Cultural Psychology, 44*(1), 122–159.

Phinney, J. S., & Devich-Navarro, M. (1997). Variations in bicultural identification among African American and Mexican American adolescents. *Journal of Research on Adolescents, 7*, 3–32.

Raske, M. (2010). Nursing home quality of life: Study of an enabling garden. *Journal of Gerontological Social Work, 53*(4), 336–351.

Rowles, G. D. (1983). Place and personal identity in old age: Observations from Appalachia. *Journal of Environmental Psychology, 3*, 299–313.

Sandstrom, G. M., & Dunn, E. W. (2014). Social interactions and well-being: The surprising power of weak ties. *Personality and Social Psychology Bulletin, 40*, 910–922.

Schwartz, S. J., & Unger, J. B. (2010). Biculturalism and context: What is biculturalism, and when is it adaptive? *Human Development, 53*, 26–32.

Schwartz, S. J., & Zamboanga, B. L. (2008). Testing Berry's model of acculturation: A confirmatory latent class approach. *Cultural Diversity and Ethnic Minority Psychology, 14*, 275–285.

Seo, Y. K., & Mazumdar, S. (2011). Feeling at home: Korean Americans in senior public housing. *Journal of Aging Studies, 25*, 233–242.

Smith, E. J. (1991). Ethnic identity development: Toward the development of a theory within the context of majority/minority status. *Journal of Counseling and Development, 70*, 181–188.

108 Building a sense of home in a foreign land

Tajfel, H., & Turner, J. (1979). An integrative theory of intergroup conflict. In W. G. Austin & S. Worchel (Eds.), *The social psychology of intergroup relations* (pp. 33–47). Monterey, CA: Brooks/Cole.

Ting-Toomey, S. (2005). Identity negotiation theory: Crossing cultural boundaries. In W. B. Gudykunst (Ed.), *Theorizing about intercultural communication* (pp. 211–233). Thousand Oaks, CA: Sage.

Trang, A. (2008). What older people want: Lessons from Chinese, Korean, and Vietnamese immigrant communities. *Generations, 32*(4), 61–63.

Vivero, V. N., & Jenkins, S. R. (1999). Existential hazards of the multicultural individual: Defining and understanding cultural homelessness. *Cultural Diversity & Ethnic Minority Psychology, 5*, 6–26.

Wahl, N-W., & Oswald, F. (2010). Environmental perspectives on ageing. In D. Dannefer & C. Phillipson (Eds.), *The Sage handbook of social gerontology* (pp. 111–124). London: Sage.

Ward, C. (2008). Thinking outside the Berry Boxes: New perspectives on identity, acculturation and intercultural relations. *International Journal of Intercultural Relations, 32*, 114–123.

Ward, C., & Lin, E-Y. (2010). There are homes at the four corners of the seas: Acculturation and adaptation of overseas Chinese. In M. H. Bond (Ed.), *The Oxford handbook of Chinese psychology* (pp. 657–677). Hong Kong: Oxford University Press.

Wiles, J. L., Leibing, A., Guberman, N., Reeve, J., & Allen, R. E. S. (2012). The meaning of "aging in place" to older people. *The Gerontologist, 52*(3), 357–366.

Zhou, M. (2014). Segmented assimilation and socio-economic integration of Chinese immigrant children in the USA. *Ethnic and Racial Studies, 37*, 1172–1183.

Index

Note: Page numbers in italic indicate a figure on the corresponding page.

acculturation 70, 93, 95–98, 102–106;
and ageing 1, 12, 15; as a home-
building process 5–9; and
transnational place 77, 87–89
ageing 1–2; challenges for older
migrants 2–5

Baffoe, M. 9
Bélanger, E.: and M. Verkuyten 77
belonging 27, 92–96, 98–99, 103–105;
and ageing 1–4, 6–12; and place
37–40, 47, 51; and relationships
55–56, 59–62, 68–69; and
transnational identity 78–82; and
transnational place 73–74, 84, 87–89
Berry, J. W. 5–6, 95–97
Bicultural Identity Integration (BII) 96
biculturalism 6, 93, 96–97, 105
Blunt, A.: and R. Dowling 9
Braun, V.: and V. Clarke 31
Brisbane 25–26, 31, 44, 63, 67–68,
84; Chung Tian Temple 66; potato
crackers in 83
Buddhism 66, 70
Buffel, T. 12
Burris, M. see Wang, C.
buses 46, 48, 51; bus stations 46, 59

Castles, S. 19
Cathay Community Association 101
Chinatowns 32–34, 94; Chinatown
Melbourne 22, 23; diaspora and
22–26
Chinese Exclusion Act 94
Chong, M. D. see Li, W. W.

chopsticks 62
Chung Tian Temple see Brisbane
church 26, 64–65, 70, 84–85
Clarke, V. see Braun, V.
Coleman, T.: and R. Kearns 45
collectivism 57
colonisation 73
community 2–4, 11–15, 26–29,
32–33, 59–60, 68–74; age-friendly
13; and building a sense of home
93–94, 99–101; transnational
74–78, 86–87; see also community
associations
community associations 44–46, 70, 82,
101, 100
Confucianism 5, 56–57, 63
Cristoforetti, A.: and colleagues 39–40,
43
culture 20; and ageing 2, 4, 6, 8–9,
11–12, 14–15; and building a sense
of home 92, 95, 99–103, 106;
cultural identification 23, 27, 32,
50, 77–79, 99; food culture 67,
81; heritage culture vii–ix, 13, 73,
76, 87, 94, 96, 104; host culture
3, 5, 33–34, 57, 69, 77, 87–89,
93, 96–97, 105; and place 48–50;
and relationships 70–71; and
transnational place 75, 79–82

Devich-Navarro, M. see Phinney, J. S.
diaspora 32–33, 73–75, 77, 105–106;
and Chinatowns 22–26
dim sum 25, 67
Dowling, R. see Blunt, A.

110 *Index*

environmental gerontology *see* theory

Erikson, E. 95–96

family 2–5, 8–9, 14–15, 98, 103–104; family care 5, 20, 63; and place 48–49; and social and cultural insideness 55–63, 67, 69–71; and transnational place 77, 79–82

filial piety 5, 9, 56–57, 63, 70–71

food vii, 9, 15, 49, 55, 63–65; and transnational place 79–81, 83–84; *see also* dim sum; potato crackers; yum cha

friends 11, 27, 56–59, 61, 63–70, 98; and place 43–46, 50; and transnational place 74, 81–82, 84–86, 88

gardens 38, 40–45, *41*, 47, 50–51, 99–100

Gardner, P. J. 59

Goffman, E. 76

Gold, S. J. 28–29

Gold Rush 20, 23–24, 32

green spaces 40–47, 51, 99–100

Hall, S. 75–76, 105

home-building process 14–15, 27–28, 32, 87, 97–98, 104; acculturation as 5–9

house 8, 29–30, 40–43, 45, 47–50; and building a sense of home 92, 98, 101; Queenslander-style *7*; and relationships 55–56, 58–61, 68; and transnational place 78, 80–82, 85, 88

identity 23, 27–28, 30–33; and ageing 1–4, 6–12, 14–15; and building a sense of home 92–98, 102–106; and place 46, 48–50; and relationships 55–57, 59, 65, 69; transnational 78–82, 86; and transnational place 73–77, 87–89; *see also* place identity

immigration 2, 4, 14, 19–22, 24, 27, 50; and building a sense of home 94, 103; and relationships 58, 61, 70; and transnational place 75, 78

individualism 57

insideness, autobiographical 11–12, 73–74, 87–89, 92; and Chinese diaspora 74–78; and transnational

identity 78–82; and transnational practice 82–86

insideness, physical 11, 37–38, 51–52, 89, 92; and green spaces 40–46; and material objects 47–51; and place attachment 38–40; and place identity 38–40

insideness, social and cultural 11–13, 55–56, 69–71, 89, 92; and family relationships signifying home 60–64; and family and social relationships 56–60; and social relationships signifying home 64–69

integration 5–6, 11, 13, 24, 52; and building a sense of home 93, 96–97, 99, 102–103, 105–106; and relationships 56, 70; and transnational place 75, 89

iPad 85–86, *86*

Jenkins, S. R. *see* Vivero, V. N.

Kearns, R. *see* Coleman, T.

Kim, C. *see* Park, H-J.

language 21, 23–24, 28, 31, 33; and ageing 8–9, 13, 15, 18; and building a sense of home 94–96, 99, 103–104; language barriers 1–4, 58, 103; and relationships 59, 63, 66, 70; and transnational place 73, 75, 79–81, 85, 87, 89

Li, W. W.: and M. D. Chong 104

Liu, L. 8

Liu, S. 9, 49

locality 93–95, 106

material objects 39–40, 47–51, 98, 100

Melbourne: Chinatown *22*, 23, 25–26

methodology *see* research

migration viii, 30, 32–34, 87–88, 94–95; and ageing 1–2, 12–13, 15; Chinese migration to Australia 20–22; *see also* immigration

multiculturalism 21, 76

neighbours 11, 29, 56–60, 68–70, 101

Neville, S.: and colleagues 13

object *see* material objects

Ottoni, C.: and colleagues 3

Index 111

Park, H-J.: and C. Kim 4
person-environment model 9–14, 37, 51, 92, 97
Phinney, J. S.: and M. Devich-Navarro 97
place *see* place, transnational; place attachment; place identity
place, transnational 71, 73–74, 87–89; and Chinese diaspora 74–78; and transnational identity 78–82; and transnational practice 82–86
place attachment 17, 37–39, 43, 46–47, 51–53, 99; and ageing 3; and relationships 55, 61
place identity 37–40, 43, 51–52, 61, 99
Proshansky, H. 38–39

Raske, M. 44, 99
relationships *see* community; family; friends; neighbours; social networks
research 1–3, 14–16, 19–20, 32–34; and acculturation 5–9; and building a sense of home 92–93, 95–101, 105–106; context of 20–26; data analysis 31–32; directions for further research 102–104; methodology 26–31; and place 37–39, 44, 51–52; and relationships 58–59; and transnational place 76–77; *see also* person-environment model
Rowles, G. 10–12, 51, 92, 98

Siu, L. 77
smartphones 77, 85–86, *86*, 88, 103
social networks 29, 44, 56, 58–60, 64–65, 68–71; and ageing 1–3, 11,

13–14; and building a sense of home 95, 98, 103–104; and transnational place 73, 75, 77, 80, 83, 85
suburbs 25–26, 59, 67, 82
supermarkets 13, 67, 82–84, *83*, 100
Sydney 23, 25, 74

tea *25*, 64, 67, 85
technology *see* iPad; smartphones
temples 65, *66*, 70, 84
theory 102; environmental gerontology 10, 12–15, 51, 97–98, 104; identity negotiation 76–77, 89, 105–106; implications of present research for 95–99; intercultural communication 104; *see also* acculturation
Ting-Toomey, S. 76, 105–106
tradition 4, 8, 20, 63, 87; and building a sense of home 94, 99, 105; Confucian 56, 63; and place 40, 45; *see also* chopsticks; yum cha
transportation 59, 67, 101; *see also* buses

Van der Does, P. 29
van Hees, S.: and colleagues 29, 51–52
Verkuyten, M. *see* Bélanger, E.
Vivero, V. N.: and S. R. Jenkins 94

Wang, C.: and M. Burris 29
White Australia policy 21, 23, 33, 76
Wiles, J. L.: and colleagues 13–15, 65, 98–99
World Health Organisation (WHO) 13

yum cha *25*, 64

Printed in the United States
by Baker & Taylor Publisher Services